THE MYSTICS OF
THE CHURCH

by EVELYN UNDERHILL

SCHOCKEN BOOKS · NEW YORK

First SCHOCKEN *edition 1964*

Second Printing, 1971

This edition is published by arrangement with
James Clarke & Co., Ltd., London

Library of Congress Catalog Card No. 64-22607

Manufactured in the United States of America

CONTENTS

PREFACE

PREFACE

SINCE any real attempt to give an account of the Mystics of the Church must involve in the end a history of personal religion in its most intense form, and its relation to the corporate Christian life, it is obvious that such an undertaking would need many years, many volumes, and much deep knowledge of the human soul. This little book can only hint at the richness and variety of the material with which anyone who tries to tell the spiritual history of the Christian Church will have to deal. It does not even claim the completeness of a catalogue; but selects from among the vast company of mystical saints a few of those whose greatness is most closely connected with their dependence on, and contribution to, the family life of the household of faith.

I have therefore left on one side the mystical philosophers, those mystics who are chiefly remarkable for their ecstatic or visionary experiences, and those spiritual individualists who have rebelled against the institutional side of religion. It is the mystic in his relation to the Church who is here considered; the great creative soul whose special experience of God does something for his fellow-Christians, who deepens the corporate spiritual consciousness, brings in fresh news about eternal life. Mysticism of this sort is and has ever been essential to Christianity, and no account of the Church's life which ignores it can claim to be complete.

Nothing perhaps has so much conduced to the misunderstanding and discrediting of the mystics as the tendency to isolate them from the Church in which they appear; to regard them as the representatives of a type of religion hostile to all ceremonial worship; and to emphasize the abnormal features of their spiritual experience. I have tried in this little survey to suggest another, and I believe a more accurate, view of their characteristics and their vocation. Limitations of space have made any detailed treatment of individuals impossible. Those who wish to continue the study of any period or group will find a short list of authorities at the end of each chapter. For convenience of reference English translations are always quoted where these exist.

E. U.

THE MYSTICS OF THE CHURCH

CHAPTER I

INTRODUCTORY

" Mystic " and " Mysticism " are words which
meet us constantly in all books that deal with
religious experience ; and indeed in many books
which do not treat of religion at all. They are
generally so vaguely and loosely used that they
convey no precise meaning to our minds, and have
now come to be perhaps the most ambiguous
terms in the whole vocabulary of religion. Any
vague sense of spiritual things, any sort of symbolism, any hazily allegorical painting, any poetry
which deals with the soul—worse than that, all
sorts of superstitions and magical practices—may
be, and often are, described as " mystical." A word
so generalized seems almost to have lost its meaning ;
and indeed, not one of these uses of " Mysticism "
is correct, though the persons to whom they are
applied may in some instances be mystics.

Mysticism, according to its historical and psychological definitions, is the direct intuition or experience
of God ; and a mystic is a person who has, to a
greater or less degree, such a direct experience—

one whose religion and life are centred, not merely on an accepted belief or practice, but on that which he regards as first-hand personal knowledge. In Greek religion, from which the word comes to us, the *mystæ* were those initiates of the " mysteries " who were believed to have received the vision of the god, and with it a new and higher life. When the Christian Church adopted this term it adopted, too, this its original meaning. The Christian mystic therefore is one for whom God and Christ are not merely objects of belief, but living facts experimentally known at first-hand ; and mysticism for him becomes, in so far as he responds to its demands, a life based on this conscious communion with God. It is found in experience that this communion, in all its varying forms and degrees, is always a communion of love ; and, in its perfection, so intimate and all-pervading that the word " union " describes it best. When St. Augustine said, " My life shall be a real life, being wholly full of Thee," he described in these words the ideal of a true Christian mysticism.

Such a general definition as this evidently needs much more explanation if we are to grasp all that it means. It shows us that mysticism represents the very soul of religion ; that it is, in fact, another name for that which is sometimes called the " spiritual life," and that no Church in which it is not present truly lives. Not only the act of contemplation, the vision or state of consciousness in which the soul of the great mystic realizes God, but many humbler and dimmer experiences of prayer, in which the little human spirit truly feels the presence of the Divine Spirit and Love, must be included in it. We cannot say that there is a separate " mystical sense," which some men have and some have not, but rather that every human soul has a certain latent capacity for God, and that in some this capacity is realized with an astonishing richness. Such a realization may be of many kinds and degrees—personal or impersonal, abrupt and ecstatic, or peaceful and continuous. This will depend partly on the temperament of the mystic, and partly on his religious background and education.

If we take all these experiences together— appearing as they do wherever religion becomes a living interest to men—we find that they are, as a matter of fact, the actual foundations on which all the great faiths are built. All the knowledge of God which is possessed by men has come to us in the last resort through some human consciousness of Him. Each great religious tradition, when we follow it back, is seen to originate in the special experiences of some soul who has acted as the revealer of spiritual reality ; for the great mystics never keep their discoveries to themselves—they have a social meaning, and always try to tell others what they have known. Thus at the root o Mohammedanism we find that it was a direct intuition and revelation of the Eternal, a vivid mystical experience, which made Mohammed the Prophet of the One God ; and the spiritual content of his message has been re-affirmed through the centuries by the Sūfi saints. So, too, the Christian Church, rooted in history and fed by experience, has been renewed again and again by the fresh contacts of its mystics with God. " I desire," said the great Ruysbroeck, " to be by the grace of God a life-giving member of Holy Church " ; and no words could express more perfectly what the office of the mystics ought to be. Their work within the religious family is to supply, and keep on supplying, the prophetic element of religion : the ever life-giving consciousness of God and His presence in and with man. We might indeed call them the eyes of the Body of Christ. They maintain that awestruck outlook towards the Infinite, and that warmly loving sense of God's indwelling grace, without which all religious institutions quickly become mechanical and cold. More than this, their vivid first-hand experience urges them to a total consecration to the service of God and of men. In them the life of prayer informs the life of action : their contemplation of Reality makes all that they do more real. Thus they show what Christian spirituality can be, and what a contribution it can make to the corporate life. By communion with them, the merely active Christian can realize the actuality of the world of spirit, and even catch something of their fire.

The mystics are the greatest of all teachers of prayer, and of that deeper communion to which disciplined prayer can lead. This they can do because of their solid hold upon unseen realities in which, at best, most of us merely " believe." In an experience which often transcended all their powers of expression, they realized God as an abiding Fact, a living Presence and Love ; and by this their whole existence was transformed. And this happened to them, not because He loved and attended to them more than He does to us ; but because they loved and attended to Him more than we do. When we read the words of St. Augustine : " I entered, and beheld with the eye of the soul the Light that never changes ; above the eye of the soul, above my intelligence " ; or when Angela of Foligno says : " I beheld the ineffable fullness of God, but I can relate nothing of it, save that I have *seen* the fullness of Divine Wisdom, wherein is all goodness " ; or St. Catherine of Siena : " I now *know for certain*, Eternal Truth, that Thou wilt not despise the desire of the petitions I have made unto Thee" ; or St. Catherine of Genoa, " If I could only show you a tithe of that Love in which I dwell ! "—we feel ourselves to be in the presence of an actual experience, so far surpassing common levels of feeling that it eludes both the subject's powers of speech and ours of apprehension.

It is obvious that since the Reality of God transcends all human conceptions, there is room for many differing types of mystical experience, and all will be incomplete. Sometimes the experience seems by reason of its strangeness dim and formless ; sometimes rich, personal, vivid. The books which the mystics write represent their efforts to tell us about it and teach us to share it : and if we read these books with sympathy and a humble effort to understand, we shall find that they do tell or at least suggest to us something of the " mighty Beauty " which these great lovers of God have known. As artists and musicians, able to see and hear created beauty to which average eyes and ears are closed, interpret and express some of it for us in their works and so give us a new vision of the world ; so the great mystics, who are geniuses in the sphere of religion, show to us the uncreated beauty of spiritual realities which we cannot find alone, and form a great body of witness to humanity's experience of God. In reading them, as in reading great poetry, we are taken out of ourselves, and become aware of deep regions of truth and beauty still beyond our reach. The Reality they are trying to show us is the same Reality which is the object of our faith ; but we see " through a glass darkly," and they, in their best moments, face to face.

It is only this view of the mystics, as people who see and experience more vividly a Reality which is there for us all, that can bring us into brotherly relation with them, and so help us in our own lives. So long as we regard them as spiritual freaks, practising some intense and esoteric sort of religion opposed to that which is sometimes called " practical Christianity," they will remain foreign to us ; and we shall miss our share of that life and light, that special knowledge of God and of the soul's relation to Him, which it is their first business to bring into the world. But if we receive their messages with the sympathy and humility which we must bring to all works of art that we desire to understand, then they will increase our religious sensitiveness, give to us a new standard and incentive in prayer, and initiate us, at least in some degree, into the veritable " riches of the House of God."

The classic Christian writers say that all our knowledge of God comes to us from three sources. First, He is manifested in the natural world and its creatures ; and realization of this is " natural theology." Next, He has declared Himself to us in history ; in many varying degrees, but supremely in and through the Christian revelation. This aspect of truth is expressed in " dogmatic theology." Last, He is found through the soul's secret and direct experience ; and this is called " mystical theology." For the fullest development of our spirits, a complete all-round religious life, we need something of all these three factors. We must learn to see and adore God's immanent presence in nature ; we must draw near to His perfect self-expression in the historic Christ ; we must seek Him at first-hand in the life of prayer. But it is only by this third aspect of religion, the cultivation of the secret inner life, that we can hope fully to enter into the other two. Without what might generally be called a prayerful disposition of mind, neither God's revelation in nature nor the teaching and practices of the Church can mean or do much for our souls. Therefore we must learn from the mystics, the great artists of that inner life, if we wish to grow up into mature men and women of God.

The history of mysticism in the Church is the history of the reaction of many different temperaments to one Reality and one demand. Thus it is a varied history, as anything so closely concerned with human character is bound to be. It does not put before us one particular kind of experience or one uniform type of perfection. Francis and Richard Rolle, full of poetry and music ; Catherine, the tanner's daughter ; Ignatius, the aristocratic soldier ; John of the Cross, the peasant saint ; Teresa, the cloistered celibate ; Lucie Christine, the devoted mother and wife; Boehme, the working cobbler ; Fénelon, the courtly priest : they all form one family and all go the same way. We find defenders of orthodoxy and initiators of heresy, deep thinkers, vivid writers, passionate lovers, vigorous men of action, organizers, parents of spiritual families, and solitary souls. But a man or woman who is to rank among the mystics of the Church must have some channel of self-expression, must be a God-possessed and life-giving personality within the corporate religious scheme.

We must not be afraid to admit that some of the experiences, actions, and conceptions which we find among the mystics were excessive and distorted ; that they were sometimes affected by mistaken views both of divine and human nature, or attributed spiritual value to emotion of a lower kind. This is one reason why mysticism so greatly needs to be tested and corrected by the general good sense of the Church, and so often tends to extravagance when divorced from it. A mystic is not necessarily a perfect human being ; and the imperfections and crudities of his character or outlook may influence and mingle with his mysticism. He may at times be feverishly emotional, or lacking in genial appreciation of his fellows ; he may be too narrowly intense, combative, intolerant. In Mechthild of Magdeburg, Richard Rolle, George Fox, we see traces of some of these failings.

It is true that the nearer the mystic draws to God, the more that meekness and love which He always awakens in the soul will triumph over these faults of character. Still, something of the natural disposition will often remain, and must be taken into account by us. These human inequalities affect the self-expression of the mystic, and help to produce that variety of type which makes Christian history so rich and so interesting. They warn us, too, against the error of over-simplification, of trying to reduce mysticism to a single and identical experience. This experience will vary in the degree in which human beings vary ; that is to say, it will exhibit the freshness and intricacy, the infinitely graduated responses, characteristic of all real life.

In reading the mystics, then, we must be careful not to cut them out of their backgrounds and try to judge them by spiritual standards alone. They are human beings immersed in the stream of human history ; children of their own time, their own Church, as well as children of Eternal Love. Like other human beings, that is to say, they have their social and their individual aspects ; and we shall not obtain a true idea of them unless both be kept in mind.

A. On the historical side, every mystic is profoundly influenced by his environment, and cannot be understood in isolation from it. He is rooted in the religious past of his race, its religious present surrounds and penetrates him whether he will or no, and through this present and this past some, indeed much, of his knowledge of God must come. However independent, however " direct " the revelation he has received, careful investigation shows how much, as a matter of fact, he owes to his spiritual ancestry, his reading, the influences that have shaped his early life. Were he indeed the lonely soul he sometimes likes to think himself, he would have no significance for his fellow-men, and such a term as " the mystics of the Church " would be meaningless. But even where he is in opposition to the external Church-life of his period—as he often is to a greater or less degree—he yet remains in a wider sense the debtor, indeed the child of the Church. The common food of the great Christian family sustains him ; and he is obliged to use its common language if he wants to be understood. From it come, ultimately, most of his conceptions ; and where he remains by choice within the institution, the beneficent effects of the corporate life, the help given him by tradition, are strongly marked.

As the life and growth of the Church proceed, her corporate consciousness, enriched by all the discoveries of the saints, grows richer : so that she has more and more to give to each of her sons. The beautiful interdependence of all Christian souls, living and dead, everything that is meant by the doctrine of the " Communion of Saints," is here strongly illustrated ; and refutes the common idea that mysticism is individualistic, and can flourish independently of history or tradition. Thus all Christian mysticism is soaked in the language and ideas of the Bible ; is perpetually taught and re-taught by St. Paul and St. John. In addition to this, it reflects the special religious colour of the period to which it belongs, and hands on to a later time the spiritual treasures extracted from it. The Catholic mystics of the Middle Ages have the peculiar beauties of their epoch, and frequently in their sayings remind us of the very spirit of

Gothic art. After the Reformation, another mood and attitude predominate, yet the link with the past is not really broken. Even such one-sided mystics as the Quakers, who hold that all truth is revealed directly by the Inner Light of God in the soul, or the Quietists, who try to wait in a blank state of passivity for His message, still depend for their most characteristic notions on the deep common beliefs of Christendom concerning God and His communion with the spirit of man.

The corporate side of Christian mysticism has therefore great importance. If we want really to understand its literature, its history, and especially its psychology, we cannot afford to neglect the influence of that great and growing body of spiritual truth on which, knowingly or not, each successive mystic feeds his soul. In all religious experience, a large part is and must be played by that which psychologists call " apperception." By apperception is meant the fact that there are in all our experiences two distinct factors. There is first the apprehension, the message, which comes to us from the outside world ; secondly there are the ideas, images and memories already present in our minds, which we involuntarily combine with the message, and by which we develop, modify or explain it. Now this mixture of perceptions and memories obviously takes place in all mystical experience. The mind which the mystic brings to his encounter with God is not a blank sheet. On the contrary, it is generally richly furnished with religious ideas and metaphors, and trained to special kinds of religious practices, all of which help him to actualize the more or less obscure apprehensions of Eternal Truth that come to him in his contemplations. Were it not so, he could hardly tell us anything of that which he has felt and known. Thus it is that certain symbols and phrases—for instance, the Fire of Love, the Spiritual Marriage, the Inward Light, the classic stages of the soul's ascent—occur again and again in the writings of the mystics, and suggest to us the substantial unity of their experiences. These phrases lead us back to the historical background within which those mystics emerge ; and remind us that they are, like other Christians, members of one another, and living (though with a peculiar intensity) the life to which all Christians are called.

B. So much for Christian mysticism in its corporate aspect ; that great continuing fact of first-hand spiritual religion, first-hand communion with God, which has never failed to vitalize the Church within which it appears. But of equal importance for us is its individual aspect : the form which it takes, the effects it produces, in the souls of the mystics themselves.

Mysticism has been defined as " the science of the Love of God," and certainly those words describe its essence. But, looking at it as it appears in the Christian Church in all its degrees and forms, I would prefer to call it " the life which aims at union with God." These terms—life, aim, union —suggest its active and purposive character ; the fact that true Christian mysticism is neither a philosophic theory nor a name for delightful religious sensations, but that it is a life with an aim, and this aim is nothing less than the union of man's spirit with the very Heart of the Universe.

INTRODUCTORY

That more or less vivid experience of God which may come early in the mystic's career, and always awakens a love and a longing for Him, is, so to speak, only the raw material of real mysticism. It is in the life and growth which follow upon this first apprehension, the power developed, the creative work performed, that we discover its true value and its place in the economy of the spiritual world.

All life, as we know, involves growth. It begins in a small way, changes, develops to maturity. It is greatly affected by its surroundings, needs food and shelter, expresses itself in varied responses and activities. It is creative, can become the parent of new life.

These characters, easily seen in the life of the natural world, are equally true of the life of the spiritual world. The life of the mystic develops from small beginnings, and passes through successive stages of growth, marked by different types of response to its spiritual surroundings. Mystics need food for their souls, and this they get from prayer and reading, from their silent contemplation of God, and frequently from the sacraments of their Church—for the idea that the typical Christian mystic is a religious free-lance, independent or contemptuous of tradition and organized worship, is, as we shall afterwards see, an illusion.

Finally, mystics are truly creative. Through their lives, deeds, and teachings, they are great sources of new spiritual life ; they gather disciples, and constantly become, as it were, the fathers or mothers of spiritual families. It was his intense mystical life in Christ which made St. Paul the real parent of the first Christian Churches ; so that it was in no merely metaphorical sense that he called them his "little children," of whom he had "travailed in birth." No one can read the Epistle to the Romans without realizing what that life-giving life had meant to him or what it had cost ; and we could say the same of St. Francis, St. Teresa, George Fox, Wesley, and many more.

Thus by Christian mysticism we mean a conscious growing life of a special kind : that growth in "Love, true Being, and creative spiritual Personality" which has been described as the essence of holiness. This life does not involve an existence withdrawn from common duties into some rapturous religious dreamland, which many people suppose to be mystical. The hard and devoted life of some of the greatest mystics of the Church at once contradicts this view. It is a life inspired by a vivid and definite aim ; the life of a dedicated will moving steadily in one direction, towards a perfect and unbroken union with God. Whatever form the experience of the mystics took—whether expressed in the deep peace of contemplative prayer or in ecstasy and other "abnormal ways"—at bottom all comes down to this. They felt, or rather feel —for there are plenty of them in the world to-day —an increasing and overwhelming certainty of first-hand contact with God, penetrating and trans-figuring them. By it they were at once deeply humbled yet intensely stimulated : it became, once for all, the supreme factor in their lives, calling forth a total response from mind, feeling and will.

Such an experience, though not peculiar to Christianity, has taken within the Christian Church a special form which is not found elsewhere. There are, of course, two distinct but complementary currents in Christian feeling and worship. One is directed towards God, the Eternal and Infinite Spirit ; the other towards His incarnate revelation in Jesus Christ. These two strains are reflected in Christian mystical experience. On the one hand, we have a group of mystics of whom St. Augustine and St. Catherine of Genoa are supreme types, whose dominant spiritual apprehension is of the absolute Being of God, and of the soul's union with Him. In technical language, they are " theocentric." God is realized by them under more or less impersonal symbols, and especially as Light and Love. " What," says St. Augustine, " do I love when I love Thee ? It is a certain light that I love, and melody, and fragrance and embrace, that I love when I love my God." Mystics of this temperament often show close correspondences with the experience of other great lovers of God, outside the Christian fold. This should not surprise us ; for since God is one, and " is not far from any one of us," there must be a common element in our limited human apprehension of Him.

On the other hand, the inner life of many of the most ardent Christian mystics is controlled by their sense of a direct personal communion with our Lord : they are " Christocentric," and can say with Walter Hilton that for them " God, grace and Jesus are all one." Within that consciousness of God as the eternal and abiding Reality, which is perhaps *the* mystic sense, this type of religious experience apprehends the intimate presence here and now of a personal Love, identified by them with the Risen and Exalted Christ, and accepted as the Master, Companion, and Helper of the soul.

Christianity is unique among the world's great religions in this : that its Founder is to His closest followers not merely a prophet, pattern of conduct, or Divine figure revealed in the historic past, but the object here and now of an experienced communion of the most vivid kind. Christians claim that this communion has continued unimpaired for nineteen hundred years, and is the true source of the Church's undying energy. Those persons who have—in continuous succession since the first Easter—most vividly experienced this, have been the means of making the Church's loyalty to her Master a living thing. These people are properly to be called mystics ; for believers in the Incarnation must, with the Fourth Evangelist, regard their apprehension as an apprehension of God in Christ. As Fénelon observes : " The Word, when He speaks to us in the state of prayer as Incarnate, must be heard with as great attention as when He speaks without representing to us His Incarnation."

Plainly, then, the lovely mediæval cult of the Holy Name, and that which is sometimes called the Evangelical experience, are alike mystical in character. Indeed, it is only by depth, intensity, and closeness that we can distinguish from these types of personal religion the intercourse claimed by the great Christocentric mystics, such as St. Catherine of Siena or Richard Rolle. The same must be said in respect of the sacramental experience through which some of the most apparently abstract contemplatives, among them Ruysbroeck and St. Catherine of Genoa, have actualized and supported their vividly personal sense of communion with God. This, too, differs in degree rather than in kind from that which nourishes the religious life of myriads of simple souls.

These two streams of feeling—in technical language, the theocentric and the Christocentric tendencies—actualized in varying degrees and proportions by fervent and contemplative spirits, make together the mystical consciousness of the Church. Within that atmosphere of spirit which is the essence of religion, this consciousness swings, as it were, between the poles of two great experiences : the transcendent and the incarnate manifestations of God. Historically these experiences are derived, the first through St. Augustine from Greek, the second through St. Paul from New Testament, sources. Psychologically they represent in their extreme forms the complementary reactions of two different types of mind to the grace of God.

In the individual, one or the other of them inevitably tends to predominate. But the greatest and most truly characteristic of the Christian mystics, from St. Paul onwards—among them Jacopone da Todi, our own Julian of Norwich, St. Teresa, and above all the mighty Ruysbroeck —embrace in their span both these aspects of man's fullest and deepest communion with Creative Love. In their contemplations of Eternity they can feel and know the Infinite God unincarnate, as the " onefold and Ineffable," the " Light without measure, and Goodness without Form." Yet they can love and serve Him incarnate, as the eternal and indwelling Christ. Thus including in their sweep both the historic and the unchanging manifestations of the Divine Life, they develop at their best a type of spirituality which is both lofty and homely ; penetrated through and through by the awed sense of God's Eternal Being, yet balancing this by an ardent personal devotion to, and communion with, Christ.

A word must be said in conclusion about the " mystic way " to which constant reference is made in works on mysticism. The " mystic way," with its three stages of purgation, illumination, and union, is a formula which was first used by the Neoplatonists and borrowed from them by Christian writers on the spiritual life. It describes in general terms the way in which the soul of the mystic usually develops ; and is paralleled by the other formula, " Beginner, Proficient, and Perfect," which many of the mediæval teachers preferred. We must remember that all these terms are often used by different writers in different senses, and thus become misleading if too rigidly understood.

By " purgation " is usually meant the purification of character and detachment from earthly interests, which is worked partly by the soul's own penitence and effort when it first seriously begins the spiritual life, and partly by the inflowing grace of God. Such purification always marks the early stages of mystical experience ; and is an intensive form of the difficult self-conquest to which, in some degree, all who really face the issues of life and the facts of their own nature are called. The term " purgative way " is also sometimes applied—for instance, by St. John of the Cross—to the gradual spiritualization of the mystic's prayer, especially the painful struggles and obscurities which accompany the transition from the stage of meditation on religious themes and figures to the beginnings of real contemplation.

By " illumination " is meant that peaceful certitude of God, and perception of the true values of existence in His light, which is the reward of the surrendered will : a perception which, as it grows, enters more and more deeply into the truths of religion and the meaning and loveliness of life—as when Angela of Foligno perceived that " the whole World is full of God." All artists in whom the love of beauty is greater than the love of self enjoy a measure of this illumination. These two stages are not rigidly separated. Indeed, in many mystics purification and progressive illumination are seen to go hand in hand ; for the nearer these draw to the vision of the Perfect, the more imperfections they discover in themselves.

Finally, by " union " is meant that perfect and self-forgetting harmony of the regenerate will with God which makes the full-grown mystic capable of " being to the Eternal Goodness what his own hand is to a man." Whereas in the earlier stages he saw and moved towards the life of Spirit, now he finds himself to be immersed in it, inspired and directed in all his actions by the indwelling love of God. This is the flower of the consecrated life, and often brings with it an astonishing access of energy and endurance, a power of dealing with persons and events far beyond the self's " natural " capacities—as we see in such lives of heroic action as those of the early Franciscans, St. Teresa, or the Quaker saints. This is the true " spiritual marriage" of the soul : a union with God so completely established that it persists unbroken among the distractions of the world, and often drives those who achieve it to renounce the private joys of contemplation in order to do work for God. The "prayer of union" described by St. Teresa and others is the reflection within the devotional life of this total and creative self-abandonment.

It need hardly be said that all these terms are general ; many differing degrees and sorts of attainment are subsumed under them, and they are seldom used with scientific exactitude. We must not therefore make them into a diagram to which we expect every mystic to conform, nor must the successive degrees of prayer and contemplation which many of the mystics describe to us be elevated into scientific laws. We are to deal with intensely living creatures, conditioned by temperament, history and environment, and must expect them to display the variety and freshness characteristic of all true life.

ILLUSTRATIVE WORKS

Butler, Dom Cuthbert. Western Mysticism. London, 1922.

Herrmann, W. The Communion of the Christian with God. London, 1895.

Hügel, Baron F. von. The Mystical Element of Religion. 2nd edition. London, 1923.

Inge, W. R. Christian Mysticism. London, 1899.

Poulain, A. The Graces of Interior Prayer. London, 1910.

Underhill, E. Mysticism. 10th edition. London, 1924.

CHAPTER II

MYSTICISM IN THE BIBLE

ST. PAUL

CHRISTIAN literature begins with a handful of letters written by a mystic : that is to say, with the epistles of St. Paul, the oldest books of the New Testament. Though we might well appeal to the Synoptic portrait of Jesus, as our real guarantee for that balanced life of loving communion with God and active charity to men which is the ideal of Christian mysticism—still, the Gospels as we have them are later than St. Paul's career. This means that the earliest documentary witness to Jesus Christ which we possess is the witness of mysticism ; and it tells us, not about His earthly life, but about the intense and transfiguring experience of His continued presence, enjoyed by one who had never known Him in the flesh. With St. Paul all that is most distinctive of truly Christian mysticism bursts on the world in its richest form, becomes the inspiration of his missionary labours, and is bequeathed by him to the infant community. Therefore any account of the office which the mystics fill in the Church must begin here.

Yet even at this apparent fountain-head the solidarity of mankind, the dependence of the soul, not only on God but also on other souls, shows itself. Christian mysticism has its roots in pre-Christian history. The voice which spoke to St. Paul on the road to Damascus addressed a mind steeped in the Old Testament, coloured especially by its prophetic writings, and accepting without question the prophetic claim to a first-hand experience of God. If, then, by the mysticism of the New Testament we must chiefly understand the claim of the first disciples to direct communion with the Spirit of Jesus, that mysticism contains and hands on factors already present in the highest forms of Jewish religion. It was fed by Hebrew literature, perhaps specially by the Psalms ; and the Church, basing on those psalms her own devotional life, was true to a great historic fact. Though on its philosophic side later Christian mysticism is often said to be derived from the Neoplatonists, this dependence upon Scripture is its real characteristic. From St. Augustine to Blake, all its greatest figures are emphatically " Bible Christians " ; and obscure Biblical phrases are the real sources of many of those symbols and images over which students now puzzle and dispute.

A conviction of direct communion with God— a vivid consciousness of His reality and presence —is characteristic of all the loftiest Old Testament writers, and indeed of Jewish personal religion as a whole. This conviction, present in germ even in the early non-literary prophets, with their tendency to ecstasy and trance and their merely national conception of Jehovah, becomes marked in the half-legendary stories centred on Samuel and Elijah ; where no one can miss the accent of sincerity in their descriptions of secret intercourse between the soul of the prophet and his God.

In such a verse as 1 Kings xix. 12 we surely recognize that absolute certitude which comes into the mind of the mystic through the deep quiet of his contemplation. Such experiences were the true, indeed the only possible, source of the immense demand for a genuine and not merely formal purity and righteousness which these men and their successors made on the still half-civilized Hebrew tribes of their day. Developed in the literary prophets, from Amos onwards, this implicit mysticism reaches its culmination in the First and Second Isaiah. A rich and direct consciousness of God, essentially mystical in character, inspired the great utterances of Ezekiel. The profound sense of the intercourse of spirit with Spirit is strongly marked in Jeremiah, who is perhaps the most mystical of the prophets—certainly the one who has most directly revealed to us the secrets of his own inner life.

Moreover, many of the psycho-physical peculiarities which often appear in connection with Christian mysticism—ecstasy, visions, the hearing of supernatural voices, the performance under interior compulsion of bizarre symbolic acts—seem to have been prominent in the prophets ; who become more intelligible to us when we compare them with their real successors, the mystics of the Christian Church. In the earliest stages of Hebrew prophecy, as in other primitive religions, ecstasy —supposed to involve Divine possession, but most often merely releasing subconscious intuitions and dreams of varying degrees of value—seems to have been deliberately induced, by music, dancing, and other devices. There was something dervish-like in the methods of the first " prophetic bands " ; and even after this crude stage of development was passed, many of the oracles of the great prophets appear to have been delivered in such an " inspired " or automatic state as that in which St. Catherine of Siena dictated her *Dialogue*. Though some of their accounts of visions may be regarded as a literary convention, it is certain that many represent real experiences, closely allied to those visions and voices in which the deep spiritual intuitions of the mystics are frequently expressed.

In the great dynamic vision which marks the consecration of Isaiah (Isa. vi.) we have the evident record under pictorial imagery of a mystical experience of God of the highest order.[1] Here the mysticism of the Old Testament achieves its most sublime expression. In these few verses we are able to recognize all the distinctive moments in a human soul's apprehension of the Being of God. First, the revelation of an ineffable Reality, filling and transcending all things, upon which even the highest of created spirits dare not look :

" I saw the Lord sitting upon a throne, high and lifted up, and His skirts filled the temple. Above Him stood the seraphim : each one had six wings ; with twain he covered his face, and with twain he covered his feet, and with twain he did fly."

[1] Rudolf Otto, *Das Heilige*, regards this as one of the greatest of all descriptions of man's apprehension of the Divine. We may compare the opinion of those Biblical critics who consider that it describes a heavy thunderstorm, in the course of which Isaiah became unnerved.

Then the unmeasured awe and adoration thrilling through the created Universe, and expressed in the seraphs' song :

" Holy, holy, holy is the Lord of Hosts : the fulness of the whole earth is His glory ! "

Then the abject nothingness and self-abasement of the creature, thus brought face to face with the otherness and mystery of the Eternal:

" Then said I, Woe is me ! for I am undone ; because I am a man of unclean lips, and I dwell in the midst of a people of unclean lips : for mine eyes have seen the King, the Lord of Hosts."

Then the cleansing pain which follows quickly on the vision : the immediate sense of vocation and self-offering which completes the soul's response :

" Then flew one of the seraphim unto me, having a live coal in his hand, which he had taken with the tongs from off the altar : and he touched my mouth with it, and said, Lo, this hath touched thy lips ; and thine iniquity is taken away, and thy sin purged. And I heard the voice of the Lord, saying, Whom shall I send, and who will go for us ? Then I said, Here am I ; send me " (Isa. vi. 1–8, R.V.).

This majestic passage has great historical as well as psychological importance ; for mediæval mystics, recognizing its quality, have used its images again and again. One thing only seems missing in it : the note of joyous intimacy, the tender feeling, which always mingles with the awestruck rapture of the Christian ecstatic: as we see if we compare it, for instance, with the vision which determined the vocation of St. Francis of Assisi, or with the gentle, almost ironic, accent of reproach in the voice that spoke to St. Paul on the way to Damascus. Here is the dividing line between the spiritual experiences of the Old and New Testaments. Yet if we refuse to allow that behind the visions and oracles of Hebrew prophecy there lies a genuine mystical apprehension of God, we are left without any adequate explanation of the way in which the vivid sense of His directive presence entered Hebrew religion and was maintained in it. Still more are we at a loss to understand why the intuitions of the prophet had for him such irresistible authority. But, once we acknowledge the unity of man's religious sense, we see that the reluctant Jeremiah accepting his destiny from the inward monitions of God, or Isaiah going three years barefoot and dressed as a captive at the Divine command, are the true spiritual ancestors of the apostle who " was not disobedient to the heavenly vision," and in the strength which that vision gave him created the Gentile Church.

Not only Jewish prophecy, but also Jewish poetry, has conditioned and nourished the development of the Christian mystics. The Synoptics represent our Lord Himself as deeply influenced by the poetry of the Psalms, and meeting His death with their phrases upon His lips ; and even apart from this, the continuity of feeling between the highest reaches of Jewish spirituality expressed in them and the Christian mystical temper is complete. The mystics of the Church have obtained more food and stimulus from this than from any other single literary source. From the psalmists come the expressions by which they best communicate their sense of the intimate yet uni-

versal presence of God, His indwelling light and
love ; as in Psalms xxiii., lxiii., and the wonderful
Psalm cxxxix.—above all, Psalm lxxiii., with its
fusion of abasement and loving certitude :

> So foolish was I, and ignorant :
> I was as a beast before Thee,
> Nevertheless I am continually with Thee :
> Thou hast holden me by my right hand.
> Thou shalt guide me with Thy counsel,
> And afterward receive me to glory.
> Whom have I in heaven but Thee ?
> And there is none upon earth that I desire beside Thee.

The essence of the mystical life and attitude is in
these lines.

St. Paul, then, the first and one of the greatest
of the Church's mystics, looking forward to the
great procession of Christian mystical saints and
giving them the language in which their most
sacred apprehensions were to be expressed, looks
back to the Hebrew prophets and psalmists, and
testifies to the unbroken stream of spiritual life
which quickens the Church. We recognize easily
in him the three-fold strand of the " mystic way " :
the moral struggles and purifications, the slow
self-conquest, so vividly described in Romans ;
the deep insights and illuminations characteristic
of the developing life of prayer ; the sense of
unbroken union with Christ which sustained his
immense activities ; the final achievement of that
surrender and rebirth in power in which he was
able to say " I live, yet not I." Comparison of his
epistles with the most trustworthy parts of Acts
helps us to reconstruct, at least tentatively, the
probable course of this spiritual evolution ; and in

so doing gives us a clue to the true meaning of many of his sayings, which, supposed by academic critics to be statements of doctrine, are often desperate attempts to describe or suggest his own experience.

The swift expansion in our Lord's outlook and teaching which we can trace in the Gospels, and which must be placed in the short period—perhaps less than two years—between the Baptism and the Crucifixion, stands in vivid contrast to that of His greatest follower. The conversion of St. Paul took place somewhere between the years A.D. 30 and A.D. 36. It follows from this that whether we regard Galatians (possibly A.D. 46) or 1 Thessalonians (*circa* A.D. 49) as his earliest surviving epistle, at least ten and perhaps fifteen or more years elapsed between his baptism and his appearance as a missionary apostle and organizer of the Churches. We can deduce by the methods of comparative psychology something of the way in which this period was probably spent. He was born in the early years of the century, and therefore at the time of St. Stephen's martyrdom would be about thirty years of age. An exact and well-instructed Jew, evidently possessing a marked religious temperament, his conversion was in no sense a conversion to God : the struggle which it ended had been a struggle to avoid recognizing in Jesus God's manifestation among men. The voice, the light, the certitude which changed his life, were essentially an inward revelation of this. The actual form this experience took tells us much about St. Paul's temperament; its emotional vehemence, its psychic instability. In many lives of the mystical type the moment of crisis and re-birth has been marked by the hearing of a voice, summing up and forcing on the mind the truth, the need, or the choice which the self has been trying to ignore. Thus St. Francis, at the moment which decided his vocation, suddenly heard the voice of Christ say to him, " Francis 1 go and repair My house " ; and Suso, hesitating before the sufferings demanded by complete self-abandonment to God's will, heard the bracing command, " Play the man ! " We might indeed expect that the crisis which determined St. Paul's surrender should take the form of a voice speaking, since the call of the Hebrew prophet is often thus described. Nevertheless in this, as in most great conversions, the actual experience was merely the last stage in a process begun long before. The gently ironic words, " It is hard for thee to kick against the goad ! " suggest that the pressure to which Paul at last surrendered had been long and steadily applied ; and the record in Acts gives us its probable origin, namely the events associated with St. Stephen's martyrdom. Though other onlookers at this tragedy only saw perhaps the execution of a tiresome fanatic, something in St. Paul responded to the joyful heroism and certitude of Stephen, and realized that they had an origin which lay beyond the world. We have here, in fact, the first and one of the greatest of examples of that peculiarly contagious character of Christian joy and holiness described by St. Augustine in the famous saying : " One loving spirit sets another spirit on fire." Through Stephen " gazing up into heaven " with self-forgetfulness and delight, St. Paul receives an impression which he cannot forget. His acquiescence in the martyrdom, the almost frenzied hatred of the Christians implied in the words " made havoc of the Church . . . threatenings and slaughter " (Acts viii. 3 and ix. 1)—all this seems to indicate desperate instinctive resistance to a revelation which he knew, if once accepted, would demand his life. The reaction to God or to Christ of the real mystical temperament, once it is awakened, is always that which psychology calls an all-or-none reaction. The whole impulsive nature first resists, and then, when at last the pressure becomes too strong, capitulates completely.

Of this law the conversion of St. Paul provides a perfect illustration. His initiation into the mystical life was both realistic and ecstatic in character. In all subsequent references to it he states his own distinct conviction that the Risen Jesus, who had appeared many times to the disciples, and whose continued activity with them is assumed in the last verses of St. Matthew and St. Mark, " appeared to me also," and once and for all laid hold on him—" I was *apprehended* " (Phil. iii. 12). The rest of his life was to be governed by the wonder and awe of that experience ; he was steadily " obedient to the heavenly vision," and slowly all that was involved in it unfolded, and more and more possessed and fed his soul. Henceforth, as Deissmann has well said, " At the commanding centre of St. Paul's contemplation of Christ there stands the Living One who is also the Crucified, or the Crucified who is also alive " ; and further : " There can be no doubt that St. Paul became influential in the world's history precisely by reason of his mysticism about Christ."

The violent breaking up of his resistances, the flooding of his mind with a new loyalty and love, produced in this ardent temperament intense psycho-physical effects. The impression of a dazzling light was followed by a brief functional blindness, in which he remained three days without food or drink ; marking the intensity of the crisis in which he had passed from the old to the new life. All that the war taught us of such psychic illness lights up and supports the short account in Acts of the seizure and its cure. From it St. Paul emerged—as St. Francis from his experience at S. Damiano—"another man than before," and at once began, with his natural thoroughness and ardour, to evangelize in the name of Christ ; already become for him a boundless source of energy and enthusiasm.

Since our only object here is to study the character of St. Paul's mysticism, his claim to the foremost place among the mystics of the Church, there is no need to follow out in detail his external history save in so far as it reveals his inner growth. The fact which mainly concerns us is this : in his mystical experience he breaks entirely new ground. He is the unique link between the primitive apostolic experiences of communion with the Risen Jesus and the still-continued Christocentric mysticism of the Church ; and might with some justice be called both the first of Evangelicals and first of Catholics.

We can gather pretty well from references in his letters and our knowledge of the mystical type the lines upon which his inner life developed. These letters, it is true—written with practical objects and largely addressed to groups of persons at the non-mystical levels of religious feeling—are not intended to disclose the deep secrets of his personal experience. Yet, as we become intimate with them, we begin to realize what their familiar phrases implied for the man who used them first ; and who was actually creating the forms under which, ever since, the Christian experience has been handed on. The raw material of St. Paul's mysticism was doubtless a temperament specially sensitive towards religion, unstable, given to the alternate depression and exaltation so characteristic of the type, and unable to rest in anything less than God. We may add to these general predispositions the violent upheaval and complete surrender of his conversion. But the upheaval disclosed interior conflicts as well as aptitudes ; the surrender was that of an ardent neophyte, and not of a completed saint. It placed him only at the beginning of the way. Therefore the statement in Galatians, that without discussion with his fellow-Christians, or even waiting to make the acquaintance of the apostles, St. Paul at once retreated into Arabia, carries with it its own explanation. Perhaps in imitation of what he had heard of Jesus, perhaps impelled only by the sense of his own need, he was driven into the solitude of the wilderness to face the facts of his new life and discover the will of God. Not till three years after his conversion does he make what appears to be his first visit as a Christian to Jerusalem.

It is certain that those years had been full of

difficulty and costly moral effort : all that the later mystics meant by the purgative way. The Gentile Church was not founded by a dreamy pietist, but by a vigorous man of action acquainted with human conflicts and temptations. If, over twenty years later, he could write in Rom. vii. the unequalled description of the incessant battle between his higher and lower impulses, his moral impotence when under the " Law," and the rescue effected in him by the power of Christ, what must this inward struggle have been when at its height ? We may be sure that when he speaks of the Christian process as a veritable death and re-birth to new life—and custom has blunted for us the tremendous meaning of these words—he is not merely borrowing an image from the pagan mysteries, but describing something through which he has passed. " For if we have grown into him by a death like his, we shall grow into him by a resurrection like his, knowing as we do that our old self has been crucified with him in order to crush the sinful body " (Rom. vi. 5, 6, Moffatt).

This period of self-conquest seems to have been accompanied by the development of those visionary and ecstatic tendencies which the circumstances of his conversion prove St. Paul to have possessed. We are told in Acts that while praying in the Temple at Jerusalem, he experienced an ecstasy in which knowledge of his peculiar vocation was revealed to him ; and we have his own admission that at least during this period he was subject to such visitations—apparently even in the pronounced form known to later mystics as " rapture," when the soul seems caught up beyond time and place to an immediate apprehension of reality, and consciousness of bodily life is lost.

In the violent little letter of which 2 Cor. xii. forms part, he speaks of the " abundance of revelations " or " wealth of visions " (Moffatt) which he has enjoyed; and of the persistent ill-health which accompanied them and was probably, as with many of the later mystics, a direct result of the psycho-physical strain involved in his ecstasies. If this letter, as is probable, was written about A.D. 53, then the great spiritual experience recorded in it as having occurred fourteen years before must have happened about A.D. 39 ; a likely date for the visit to Jerusalem which is described in Acts xx. 17 and Gal. i. 18.   In this passage St. Paul distinctly lays claim to a full ecstatic experience, with its special characters of a narrowed and entranced consciousness—" whether in the body or out of the body I cannot tell,"—and of ineffability, " hearing unspeakable words," or, as Moffatt translates, " sacred secrets which no human lips can repeat."

If, then, we are to obtain a true idea of St. Paul's personality and the source of his amazing powers, we must correct the view which sees him mainly as theologian and organizer by that which recognizes in him a great contemplative.   For here we have not only a sense of vivid contact with the Risen Jesus, translated into visionary terms—" I fell into a trance and saw him saying to me "—but an immediate apprehension of the Being of God, such as we meet again in St. Augustine and in certain mediæval ecstatics.

If we compare one of the later Christian mystics,

of whose development we know a good deal, with our fragmentary knowledge of St. Paul's inner life, much emerges that is of interest. One of the best examples for this purpose is St. Teresa ; for though the careers of the cloistered nun and of the unresting Jewish missionary seem at first sight to have little in common, the spiritual likeness between them is often close. Both possessed a devouring enthusiasm for God and Christ, and were subject to voices, visions and ecstatic trances. Both were persons of singular courage, energy and common sense. The mystical life of St. Teresa falls into two distinct parts. During the first she lived in much retirement in her convent ; displaying little outward initiative, but making great progress in the interior life. Towards its close she, like St. Paul, enjoyed " an abundance of revelations " and experienced the visions and ecstasies described in her *Life*. The second period—that of her active career as founder and reformer of religious houses—was marked by fewer ecstasies and visions, which were replaced by a steady inward certainty of union with God, and by a new strength and endurance, a capacity for action, which she attributed to this cause. In the conventional language of mysticism, these two stages were those of the " illuminative " and the " unitive " life.

A somewhat similar development can be traced in St. Paul. During the ten or twelve almost unchronicled years in which he remained a subordinate working in the Jewish Christian Church, he, too, as we have seen, claims to have " enjoyed visions and revelations of the Lord " (2 Cor. xii.). At this time, too, we may suppose that he was

43

faced by the task of conquering not only his own nature, but also the suspicions with which he was at first inevitably regarded (Acts ix. 26). But when his vocation definitely declared itself, perhaps about A.D. 46–47, and he " was separated by the Spirit" for the active missionary career, this mainly subjective stage of development was replaced by that deeper, more fruitful sense of total possession by the indwelling Spirit of Christ, which supported his astonishing labours and sufferings and inspired his writings. Doubtless he remained, like most men of religious genius, liable to abrupt and authoritative intuitions—what George Fox called " openings "—and also to sudden waves of fervent feeling, when he seemed " beside himself as towards God," though none the less calm and sober in his practical dealings with men (2 Cor. v. 13).

Ecstatic phenomena were almost taken for granted in the Early Church ; and St. Paul's distinction as a mystic lies not in their possession, but in the detachment with which he regarded them. Thus in A.D. 52, when he wrote his first letter to the Corinthians, he acknowledged his continued possession of the much-prized " gift of tongues "; those outbursts of ecstatic but unintelligible speech common in times of religious excitement. But his attitude toward such external " manifestations of the Spirit " is marked by a cool common sense which must amaze us when we consider the period in which he wrote, the universal respect for the marvellous, and the circumstances of his own conversion. His rule is simple. He discounts any " gifts " and experiences which do not help other souls. The mystical communion of his soul with Christ must not be a matter of personal enjoyment : it must support and not supplant the apostolic career. "Forasmuch as ye are zealous of spiritual gifts, seek that ye may excel to the upbuilding of the Church. . . . I will pray with the Spirit, *and* I will pray with the understanding too."

Therefore we misunderstand St. Paul's mysticism if we confuse it with its more sensational expressions. As his spiritual life matured his conviction of union with the Spirit of Christ became deeper and more stable. It disclosed itself, not as an interference with the natural order, but as a source of more than natural power. Its keynote is struck in the great saying of his last authentic letter : " I can do all things through Christ which strengtheneth me " (Phil. iv. 13). This statement has long ago been diluted to the pious level, and we have ceased to realize how startling it was and is. But St. Paul used it in the most practical sense, in a letter written from prison after twelve years of superhuman toil, privation, and ill-usage, accompanied by chronic ill-health ; years which had included scourgings, stonings, shipwreck, imprisonments, " in journeyings often, in perils of waters, in perils of robbers, in perils by mine own countrymen, in perils by the heathen, in perils in the city, in perils in the wilderness, in perils in the sea, in perils among false brethren ; in weariness and painfulness, in watchings often, in hunger and thirst, in fastings often, in cold and nakedness " (2 Cor. xi. 26, 27). These, and not his spiritual activities and successes alone, are among the memories which would be present in St. Paul's consciousness when he declared his ability " to do *all* things."

With this sudden phrase there enters Christian history a conception, or rather an enlargement of human experience, destined to have an influence which we can hardly over-rate. Benedict, creating single-handed the fabric of Western monasticism ; Bernard achieving the impossible at Clairvaux ; Ignatius Loyola, physically feeble, yet tramping penniless from Paris to Rome under the spur of his vocation ; Elizabeth Fry in Newgate Gaol ; Livingstone in Africa—all go back to St. Paul for a description of the actual, yet mysterious, power by which they felt themselves supported and enhanced. He was the first to experience and describe this newness of life, this self-abandoned energy and freedom, which, as he insisted, make every real Christian a " new creature," and consti- tute the essential characters of Christian mysticism properly so called. Much of the difficulty of St. Paul's " doctrine " comes from the fact that he is not trying to invent a theology, but simply to find words which shall represent to others this vivid truth—" I live, yet not I . . . to live is Christ . . . Christ *in* me. . . ." Behind his efforts to prove to recalcitrant hearers the logical nature of the Christian case, we feel the pressure of that " overflowing grace and free gift " (Rom. v. 17) which transcends argument, and must be suggested rather than declared.

If now we read even such a comparatively unmystical letter as that to the Galatians, what do we find to support our idea of Paul's mysticism ? The letter, of course, had a practical aim ; its

personal references are scattered and indirect ;
but we are made to feel that a personal experience,
and that of a unique kind, determines the writer's
whole attitude. The first sentence emphasizes
the ruling fact of his supernatural " call."   " Paul,
an apostle, not appointed by men, *but* by Jesus
Christ " ; and this vivid sense of acting always
under the direct impulsion of his Master is implied
in every line.   " It is no longer I who live : Christ
lives in me " (ii. 20). His disgust at the folly
of the Galatian converts is proportionate to the
intensity of his own religious realism.   " O senseless Galatians ! who has bewitched you ? . . .
Have you had all that experience for *nothing* ? "
(iii. 1, 4). And if we ask what this experience
has been, the magnificent outburst of the fourth
chapter answers us : it is that consciousness of
the soul's life in God which makes him " no more
a servant, but a son . . . not children of the
bondwoman, but of the *free*." A long development
lies between the young zealot's capitulation outside
Damascus, with its note of submission and awe,
and this sense of being at home in the spiritual
world. All that he says to the Galatians we may
be sure he has himself experienced ; and, with the
humility and optimism of all great spirits, believes
that they can experience too.

The period of twelve or fourteen years within
which the extant epistles were written gives time
for considerable spiritual development ; and we
can trace a distinct progress from the stress and
vehemence of St. Paul's earlier writings to that
tranquil joy and peace which mark real maturity
of soul, and are the outstanding characteristics of

Philippians. His mystical conceptions are already developed in the period of 1 Corinthians, with its great distinction between the " psychic " or intellectual, and the spiritually sensitive man, and its declaration of the hidden wisdom revealed by the immanent spirit " that searcheth *all* things ; yea, the *deep* things of God," to those who have the mind of Christ (1 Cor. ii. 10).

We notice in Romans, the typical letter of his middle period (*c*. A.D. 56), a growing sense of power, stability and freedom : a condition closely associated in St. Paul's mind with the idea of " Grace." " Grace " is for him no theological abstraction, but an actual, inflowing energy, which makes possible man's transition from the natural to the spiritual state.

Anyone who still supposes him to be predominantly a legalist should consider how profoundly supernatural a conception of Christianity underlies the opening paragraph of Romans ; what a struggle to describe the actual but subtle facts of the inner life is to be felt in its greatest passages, which often seek to suggest an experience beyond the range of common speech. This letter is the work of a man who has fully emerged into a new sphere of consciousness, has been " made free by the Spirit of Life," " a new creature," and enjoys that sense of boundless possibility which he calls " the glorious liberty of the children of God " (viii. 21). He knows the mysterious truth, which only direct experience can bring home to us, that somehow even in this determined world " *all* things work together for good to them that love God." Nor does he fail to link this grand, because selfless, confidence with the tensions and sufferings of practical life. " Who shall separate us from the love of Christ ? shall tribulation, or distress, or persecution, or famine, or nakedness, or peril, or sword ? . . . Nay, in *all* these things we are more than conquerors " (viii. 35, 37).

Power and tranquillity, then, are the fruits of St. Paul's mysticism ; sufficiently astonishing fruits in one who seems to have combined natural vehemence with considerable ill-health. He had learned, in action and in contemplation, that " to be spiritually minded is life and peace " (viii. 6). The whole secret of Christian sanctity seems to be distilled in this little phrase.

This life and peace, when we come to the latest of his surviving epistles, are found more and more to dominate the scene, bringing a power and joy which no external trials can dim. The characteristic epistle here is, of course, Philippians, written from prison, and probably from Rome, about A.D. 60 ; but the same temper of mind emerges in Colossians, which—if accepted as a genuine Pauline letter—also belongs to this period.

In these writings we recognize an ever more perfect mingling of the mystical outlook and the practical demand : of other-worldly joy, and immediate stress. Dealing with the most concrete problems, they are transfused by a spiritual glow. Almost the whole science of the inner life could be deduced from them : the paradoxical combination of self-discipline and joy ; the emphasis on humility and love ; the demand for detachment ; the developed doctrine of union with Christ as a veritable source of power (Phil. ii. 1–9 ; iii. 8 ;

iv. 13). In the technical language of mysticism, St. Paul, at full spiritual maturity, is now living the " theopathetic life," humbly yet deeply aware of the actual energy of God operative within each deed and decision of his own. By the time Philippians was written, it is plain that some at least of his converts had also reached the deeper levels of spiritual experience. Hence in iii. 15 he deliberately addresses the " perfect "—that is, those who are no longer neophytes, but have been initiated into the mysterious realities of Christian regeneration, and, drawn to the full life of consecration, press with him " towards the mark." To these he promises, as the reward of a complete self-abandonment which is " careful for nothing," that inexplicable tranquillity which abides in the deeps of the perfectly surrendered soul : the peaceful presence of the Infinite " which passeth all understanding," keeping steady guard within and beneath all fluctuations of feeling and thought.

In this phrase, I think, we reach the heart of St. Paul's mystical experience, the point in which his vivid apprehensions of the living personal Christ and of the spaceless and eternal God unite. For he is a true mystic, and the originator of the great mystical tradition of Christianity, in this : that he ever retains, in and with his ardent and realistic Christology, a profound consciousness of the Infinite, Unchanging God, Who manifests Himself in Christ. The secret experiences of his soul have compelled St. Paul to find in Christ the " Yes of God " (2 Cor. i. 20), the " pleroma of Deity " (Col. ii. 9). But his sacramental outlook, his personal consciousness of immanent Christ-spirit, are enfolded in an unmeasured transcendentalism, an awed consciousness of " the vast and stormy sea of the Divine " ; and they gain their meaning and value from this. " *God* shall be all in all ! " is his last word for the consummation for which he waits (1 Cor. xv. 28). Though the actual words of the Sermon at Athens (Acts xvii. 22–28) may not be those used by the Apostle, they are certainly true to his spiritual outlook. His God is an eternal and discoverable Presence, a boundless substance, intimate and all-controlling, near yet far, " in Whom we live and move and have our being."

Hellenistic thought, always congenial to the mystical temperament, has here added something to the loftiest intuitions of Judaism, and interpreted anew the gospel of Divine Fatherhood proclaimed by Jesus. Such a phrase as this already looks towards that Christian Platonism through which so many mystics have expressed their profoundest experiences. Its authority covers St. Catherine of Genoa's daring " My *me* is God, nor do I know my selfhood save in Him," and Ruysbroeck's " Where He comes, there He is : and where He is there He comes . . . and everything in which He is, is in Him, for He never goes out of Himself." It is this power of combining the infinite and the human aspects of God's self-revelation to men which gives St. Paul his unique importance as the first of the great mystics of the Church.

ILLUSTRATIVE WORKS

Deissmann, A.   St. Paul.   London, 1912.

Gardner, Percy.   The Religious Experience of St. Paul. London, 1911.

Moffatt, J.   The Old Testament : a new translation. 2 vols.   London, 1924.

The New Testament : a new translation.   London.

Smith, Prof. David.   Life and Letters of St. Paul.   London, 1919.

Way, A.   The Letters of St. Paul.   3rd edition.   London, 1911.

CHAPTER III

MYSTICISM IN THE EARLY CHURCH

CASSIAN—ST. AUGUSTINE—DIONYSIUS THE AREOPAGITE

IT is certain that the Christian Church has never been without mystics ; that is to say, persons capable of direct experience of God and of spiritual things. Yet there are periods in which this mystical instinct seems to rise to the surface of her conscious life, expressed in some great personality or group of personalities. Then it becomes articulate, and starts a fresh current of thought and feeling in respect of the infinite mysteries of God.

Any short account of the mystics of the Church must fix our attention on these landmarks. But their significance is only understood if we remember that they are not solitary beacons set up in the arid wilderness of " external religion " ; they are rather surviving records of a spiritual culture, content, for the most part, to live in secret, and leaving few memorials behind. The stretches of country between them were inhabited by countless humble spirits, capable in their own degree of first-hand experience of God. Only realizing this can we reach a true conception of the perennial richness and freshness of the Church's inner life.

Thus, the importance of St. Paul's epistles does

not abide only in their writer's mystical greatness, his unique power of describing the mysterious intercourse of the Christian soul with Christ, but also, indeed largely, in the fact that the persons St. Paul was addressing included some capable of understanding the height, breadth and depth of his utterance ; of sharing his vision and joy. This means that in the Primitive Church St. Paul's experience was not unique in kind, but only in degree. So, too, the significance of Cassian's *Dialogues*, or of the literature produced in the fourteenth century by the Friends of God, lies in the fact that they do not merely tell the experiences of one privileged spirit ; but represent and minister to the mystical demands of a whole period eager for, and able to assimilate, the secrets of the contemplative life.

Mysticism only thus becomes articulate when there is a public which craves for the mystic's message ; for except in response to the need of others, it is the instinct of every contemplative to keep his secret to himself. Thus each of our chosen landmarks witnesses to more than its own achievement ; registers an upward surge of humanity towards the things of God.

Such an upward surge—the first Christian mystical period—is recorded in the New Testament, and is dominated by the experiences of St. Paul and the Fourth Evangelist. From it comes one of the two great streams of tradition which have nourished the secret life of the Church. We can trace in the early Greek Fathers—especially Clement of Alexandria (*c.* 150–220) and his pupil Origen (*c.* 183–253), the approximate contemporary of Plotinus—the beginnings of the second stream of tradition ; that of Christian Neoplatonism. Neither of these vigorous thinkers can properly be called mystics ; we feel in both an excess of the knowledge of the head over the wisdom of the heart, a lack, too, of the heroic self-abandonment of the saints. But Christian spirituality owes them a great debt. Clement, insisting on the contemplation of God as the goal of Christian achievement, and applying the language of the Hellenic mysteries —their three grades of purification, enlightenment and union—to the growth of the contemplative soul, laid the foundations of " mystical theology." So, too, in Origen we find wonderful insights ; but hardly in either that supernatural life of action transfused by resignation, which is the mark of the self fully united to God.

Both the Montanist movement of the second century, with its unbridled cultivation of ecstatic phenomena and impossible demand for " a spiritual church of spiritual men," and the half-pagan theosophy of the Gnostics, are often brought forward as evidences of the mystical life of the Early Church. But history shows that it is never in such insistence on the abnormal that man finds the true sources of spiritual life or real communion with eternity. These movements, with their feverish exaltation, lack of balance and humility, arrogant claim to peculiar knowledge, added nothing to the Christian's experience of Reality ; nor any names to the Church's roll of honour. They are merely examples of that spurious mysticality which arises at intervals throughout Christian history. Not here, but in the sober life of prayer and union which has always been practised by thousands of humble and nameless contemplative souls, we find the continuing mystical life of the Church.

With the fourth century we reach the next significant period for the growth of Christian mysticism : when the Church, growing and groping, was bringing in new elements of Egyptian, Greek and Latin origin to actualize and enrich her inner experience, give variety and unity both to her doctrine and to her apprehension of God. Then arose the primitive monasticism of the monks and hermits of the Egyptian desert ; a great if one-sided attempt to develop the contemplative life, provide a frame within which men might live in perfect communion with, and surrender to, God. As a later mystic said of his own turning from the world, the early monk " fled that which him confused " ; and was able as the result of this simplification to give the Church new and deeper insights into spiritual things.

The early monk's excessive depreciation of natural life ought not to blind us to the truth that this was a great concerted attempt to develop through self-denial the spiritual side of human nature and advance in the knowledge of God. It was intensive : but religion would be greatly impoverished were all its intensive experiments suppressed. The heroic renunciations of the early Fathers of the Desert deeply impressed the general Christian consciousness ; as we see in those passages of St. Augustine's *Confessions* which describe how his conversion was facilitated by hearing, for the first time, the history of St. Anthony of Egypt, and of " the crowded monasteries, the ways of Thy sweetness, the teeming solitudes of the desert " which had resulted from his example and activity (*Conf.* viii. 6). And after his baptism Augustine's first thought was to retire with a few companions to Africa, and form an ascetic community of the Egyptian type. We stand here, in fact, at the fountainhead of that "mysticism of the cloister " which produced many lovely examples of the life of union with God. Along this line the psychology and discipline of the mystical life were developed, and the laws of prayer and contemplation gradually worked out. The spontaneous enthusiasm, the loving ardours of primitive Christian spirituality here submitted to a drastic—even a ferocious—education : the idea of deliberate purification and discipline, implicit in the Greek mysteries, entered the Christian scheme, and mysticism became allied for good or evil with asceticism.

Two great books reveal the spirit of this closed chapter in the history of man's spiritual evolution, and have been the channels through which the wisdom of these early monks passed to the mediæval and modern worlds. One is the *Vitæ Patrum*, a vast collection of miscellaneous material relating to the lives and sayings of the Fathers of the Desert ; the other is the celebrated *Dialogues* of Cassian, probably composed within a few years of St. Augustine's death, but dependent for its substance on a form of life already well developed in his day.

A man of much learning and holiness, the pupil of St. John Chrysostom, Cassian was born about A.D. 350, and educated at Bethlehem. In early middle age he journeyed for seven years through the Egyptian desert, visiting the great monasteries, studying their life, and conversing on spiritual things with the monks. The material thus collected forms the basis of the *Dialogues*, which, says Abbot Butler, " was the first considerable scientific exposition ever composed on the spiritual life : and it remains to this day in many respects the finest and best." All the later Christian mystics are much indebted to it. We find here the first psychological account of those moods and movements of the religious consciousness, afterwards codified as the " degrees of prayers " ; and their correspondence with the successive stages of the spiritual life. This alone gives the *Dialogues* unique importance for those who wish to understand the thoroughly historical character of Christian mysticism. Since St. Benedict wrote his rule, they have formed part of the spiritual reading of every Benedictine monk. St. Thomas Aquinas kept them always upon his desk. Their language and imagery can be recognized in the works of all the great masters of the spiritual life : and a return to their solid doctrine might do much for us.

The sober realism of Cassian's descriptions has always been appreciated by those who have had the training of souls ; and modern psychology has but endorsed their essential truthfulness. He shows the life of communion with God developing by gradual stages, which keep pace with the self's increasing purification, till it reaches that state of pure thanksgiving and adoration in which it is " lifted up with fervour of heart to a certain burning prayer which the speech of man cannot express, nor the thought of man comprehend," and at last attains "a still more sublime and exalted condition, which is brought about by the contemplation of God alone and by ardent love ; wherein the mind, as it were flung and dissolved into this love, converses with Him in utmost familiarity."

But even this ineffable experience is realized by Cassian as a means, not an end ; and is to be judged by its fruits. " When we are lifted up and established in this sublime state of *children* of God, we shall at once feel ourselves inflamed by that filial desire with which all His true children burn ; and, no longer concerned with our own selfish interests, we shall seek solely the honour and glory of our Father." Hence the essence of the monastic life, as he says in another place, consists not in pious exercises, but in a daily and hourly act of renunciation ; bringing the soul to that condition of constant and uninterrupted communion with God which is substantially identical with the "unitive way" of mysticism. "The end of all our perfection is thus so to act that the soul, stripping itself daily of all earthly and carnal inclinations, lifts itself up without ceasing more and more towards spiritual things ; that so all its works and thoughts, and all the movements of the heart, may become nothing else but a continuous act of prayer " (*Dial.* x. cap. 5).

This lofty and bracing idea of the spiritual life, not the performance of long religious exercises, still remains that which the contemplative orders of the Church set before their subjects. Many mystics have practised, none have improved upon it ; for it is consistent not only with a cloistered, but also with an active career. It involves such a genuine remaking of personality on levels of self-devotion that at last—to quote Cassian again —" all we love and desire, all we seek and wish for, all that we think and perceive, all that we speak of and hope for, is God."

But the wisdom of the Egyptian solitaries was not the only great contribution made by the fourth century to Christian mysticism. In the person and work of St. Augustine we have the second great landmark in the history of the mystics of the Church : a landmark of such importance, that fully to understand the mediæval mystics, we ought to know his *Confessions* almost by heart. The significance of St. Augustine is two-fold. First, he was a great natural mystic, with remarkable powers of self-analysis and expression ; and has left us one of the most marvellous records in history of the transmutation of a soul by the supernatural grace of God. Next, he brought Greek thought and religious feeling into the main stream of Christian mysticism, thus giving it a colour which it has never lost.

The influence of Plotinus, the great Neoplatonist and ecstatic (A.D. 204–270), was decisive for the form in which his experience of Eternal Life was to be described. Had Plotinus not been a great mystic as well as a great philosopher, his works would not have affected Augustine so much. Had Augustine not become a great mystic, he could not have filled up the Plotinian conceptions of God with the light and fire which have made them channels of revelation. It is the considered opinion of Eucken that Plotinus, who rejected

Christianity, has nevertheless influenced Christian thought more than any other writer since St. Paul : and this persistent influence of the Pagan mystic upon the spiritual development of Christendom was chiefly exercised through St. Augustine's works.

Augustine, born in North Africa in A.D. 354, by temperament a sensualist and eager taster of experience, capable of a wide range of reactions —a thirster after truth and beauty, an ardent lover and friend—was the stuff of which great converts are made. He was thirty-two when his conversion took place, in circumstances known to all readers of religious literature. The fact, and everything in the varied and uneasy life which had preceded it, are all contained in the most celebrated of his utterances—" Our hearts are restless till they rest in Thee."

The list of the lesser satisfactions of mind and sense by which he had failed to be satisfied is fully set out in the early books of the *Confessions* ; where we can trace the long three-cornered struggle between the claims of his ardent passions, his logical intellect, his deeply mystical and God-desiring soul. He shows very clearly the dependence of the mystic on environment : the extent in which all the circumstances of his life—even the most apparently unspiritual—contribute to his formation. He is not an anæmic visionary, but a whole man ; who has loved, sinned and endured, indulged his passions without remorse, and used his mental powers without humility. His vitality poured itself out in passionate appreciation of every aspect of life. His devoted friendships prove his personal attractiveness ; an attractiveness perhaps more felt by his equals than by his superiors.

The passage in the *Confessions* which shows the self-assured young professor penetrating to the presence of St. Ambrose, to find that his appearance—usually so appreciated—is not even perceived, throws an amusing light on the education of the embryo saint. Augustine's love of argument, intellectual vanity and self-absorption, expectations and disillusionments, are all exhibited in this little encounter between the restless, brilliant, conceited young don and the calm old shepherd of souls. " I could not ask him what I wanted *as* I wanted, because the shoals of busy people to whose infirmities he ministered came between me and his ear and lips. . . . Often when we attended (for the door was open to all, and none was announced) we saw him reading silently, but never otherwise, and after sitting for some time without speaking— for who would presume to trouble one so occupied ? —we went away . . . the flood of *my* difficulties could only be poured out to a listener with abundant leisure at his disposal, and such an one I could not find ! " (*Conf.* vi. 3).

Augustine's real obstacles, however, were not intellectual problems. They were difficulties of character and conduct : the tyranny of " carnal use and wont," the unresolved discord between his behaviour and his ideals, above all the paralysing sense of his own cleverness. When he wrote the *Confessions*, after nine years' experience of the spiritual life, these facts were clear to him ; and he has set them down in a series of vivid phrases. " By my swelling pride I was separated from Thee,

and my puffed-up face closed up mine eyes ! "
He longed for God, but only on his own terms
—" I wished to be as certain of things unseen, as
that seven and three make ten." He hung about
on the verge of the essential surrender—" I prayed
for purity, but not yet ! " Hence vision stopped
short of action. " I was caught up to Thee by
Thy Beauty, and dragged back by my own weight ;
and fell once more with a groan to the world of
sense. . . . I attained in the flash of one hurried
glance to the Vision of That Which Is, but I could
not sustain my gaze " (*Conf.* viii. 17).

From no other writer do we obtain so clear a
sense as that which Augustine gives us of the
direct, moulding action of Spirit upon human
life : the over-ruling Energy drawing each soul
to its own place. " I tossed upon the waves,
and Thou didst steer. . . . Thou, Lord, who
standest by the helm of all things that Thou
hast made."

Yet this mysterious guidance was exercised
through and in the things of mind and sense.
The books of the Platonists, especially the
Enneads of Plotinus with their mystical realism
and philosophic sweep, explicating the meaning of
Christian theism, began Augustine's conversion ;
turning his vague belief in God into an intense
though still largely intellectual realization. There
came a moment when " I was astonished to find
I loved Thee, my God, and no more an empty
phantom." But these dazzling glimpses were still
far from the mystics' peaceful, awestruck, and
fruitful experience of Reality. They could " show
as from a wooded height the land of peace, but

not the road thereto " : possessed no life-transforming power. With the humbling perception of this fact, Augustine realized that his difficulties were not caused by mental superiority, but by spiritual incapacity and childishness. " When first I knew Thee, Thou didst take hold of me, so that I could see there was *something* to be seen, though I was not yet fit to see it. . . . And Thou didst beat back my weak sight, dazzling me with Thy splendour, and I thrilled with love and dread ; and I perceived that I was far away from Thee in the land of unlikeness, as if I heard Thy voice from on high crying unto me—' I am the Food of the full-grown ; grow, and thou shalt feed on Me ' " (*Conf.* vii. 7 and 10). This stretching of the " narrow house of his soul " for an experience still beyond his span was set going by two agencies. First, by a new and humble discovery of Christian spirituality in the epistles of St. Paul, which he re-read at this critical moment of his career ; secondly, by the personal influence of Christian souls. Thus his achievement of God, in the end, was the direct result of historical and social contacts ; far, indeed, from the Plotinian " flight of the Alone to the Alone ! " In St. Paul Augustine discovered " that love which buildeth on humility " ; a quality of soul which Platonic philosophy cannot teach. In his mother, St. Monica, he saw and felt this love in action : and her faithful life of prayer was doubtless a chief factor in his transformation. At the right moment, the wise old priest Simplicianus told him of the conversion of Victorinus—a person whose intellect Augustine was bound to respect—and that eminent philosopher's humble profession of faith (*Conf.* viii. 1, 2). Finally, the history of St. Anthony and the Egyptian monks, told by his friend Pontitianus, roused Augustine's instinct for heroic self-donation ; forced him to realize his own unworthy refusals, the petty vileness of his past life. " Thou, O Lord, didst turn me round into my own sight. I had set myself, as it were, at my own back, because I was unwilling to see myself. And now Thou didst place me before mine own eyes, so that I beheld how ugly I was ; how deformed, filthy, spotted, and ulcerous ! " (*Conf.* viii. 7.) In that moment conceit was killed and spirituality was born.

We see by how many strands Augustine was attached to history and human existence, by how many channels the new life forced its way into his starving yet reluctant soul, how false any account of his conversion as a sudden and solitary encounter with God. The child's voice heard in the garden completed a situation long prepared.

At thirty-three years old, then—approximately the period of St. Paul's conversion—Augustine entered the mystic way, with the uncompromising completeness of a great soul. As St. Paul hid himself in Arabia, so his first desire was to leave the world in which he was so successful a figure, go back to Africa, and there lead a humble, ascetic life. He sacrificed at one blow career, tastes, passions, everything he had loved : nor did he get in exchange the quietude for which the mystic always longs. He was beset by homely and practical responsi-bilities : family ties, pupils, disciples. His chief spiritual support, the sanctity and devoted love of his mother, was removed within a year of his conversion. The wonderful scene at Ostia, described in the most celebrated section of the *Confessions* (Bk. ix. 10) suggests that St. Monica was her son's first director in the contemplative life ; that in the ascent of their souls to the fleeting experience of " the Eternal Wisdom that abides above all," it was hers, disciplined by years of self-denial and prayer, that supported and led him on. Hence the desolation caused by her death. Perhaps it is to her that he refers in *De Quantitate Animæ*, written soon after his baptism ; where, describing the last stage of the spiritual ascent, the attainment in this life of " the perfect peace and breath of Eternity," he speaks of " Certain great and incomparable souls, whom we believe to have seen, and to see, these things ; and who have told as much as they judged meet."

We see from this quotation that at the time of St. Monica's death Augustine claimed no such experience of the Vision of God, as he describes in many passages of the *Confessions*, composed at a later stage in his Christian life. This means that the nine years following his conversion witnessed the whole of that interior growth which turned the fiery and tormented convert into the solid man of prayer, able to take " the food of the full grown." They converted ardour into charity ; the desire for redemption into the desire to redeem ; the self-centred craving for God to the outflowing love which desires chiefly to impart Him. It is an Augustinian maxim that the heart of man is as great as its love : and narrowness of soul was prominent among the imperfections he discovered

in himself—" The house of my soul is narrow
—O enlarge it, that Thou mayst enter in ! "
(*Conf.* i. 5).

The conditions in which this expansion took
place were far from those supposed to be congenial
to the mystic. Increasing pressure of pastoral
and official work, constant demands on time,
thought and sympathy, trained and tested his
charity, suppleness and self-oblivion. Five years
after his conversion Augustine became, with great
reluctance, a priest and the assistant-bishop of
Hippo ; four years later, at the age of forty-one,
its bishop. His position at Hippo was not unlike
that of the overworked rector of a large city parish,
in which some new and sensational religious movement has carried off most of the congregation.
The Donatist schism had split the African Church,
and the Catholic section was the smaller and less
popular of the two. Constant controversy and propaganda were required of its bishop ; Augustine's
genius for argument and rhetoric found new scope.
Endless sermons, books, tracts against heresy,
and private letters marked his episcopate : his
inward life, like that of St. Paul, prompted to
creative work. Pauline, too, is the interest he
now developed in the corporate side of Christianity ;
for this great mystic and Platonist was the first
to define the nature of the Church, as a home for
souls and a necessary condition of the life of
grace.

Augustine, then, beginning again on fresh levels
that fullness of mental and practical life which
marked his youth, provides one of the greatest
examples of that union of action with contempla-

tion in which, as St. Teresa put it, " Martha and Mary combine."

The *Confessions* were written early in his episcopate : thus their great mystical outbursts represent his position and feeling after nine years' hard work as a member of the Church. Those years had doubtless involved extreme and purifying tension ; a constant struggle to reconcile the claims of the outer and inner life. No one less resembled the " idle contemplative " of popular imagination ; yet in no one more than in this untiring writer, preacher and administrator do we feel the vivid reality of the world of spirit, the actual flight of the soul to God.

The *Confessions*, then, contain not merely spiritual biography, but the deep meditations of a Christian mystic on his past experience. " With what fruit," says Augustine, " do I by this book before Thee confess unto men, what at this time I *now* am, not what I have been ? " (*Conf.* x. 3).

He had become, as the *Confessions* prove, a great experimental theist ; perhaps the greatest who has recorded his intercourse with God. After making every allowance for natural eloquence and the influence of Neoplatonism, none can mistake the language of first-hand experience and passionate feeling. Looking back, he sees from the beginning the steadfast pursuit of the Hound of Heaven ; the moulding action of that Love which now penetrates and supports his active life. " I fell away, and became all darkened ; yet even thence, even thence, came I to love Thee ! I went astray, and I remembered Thee. I heard Thy voice behind me, calling me to return, but scarcely could

I discern it for the noise of the enemies of peace !
And see, here I return now, sweating and panting
after Thy fountain. Let no man forbid me ;
this will I drink, thus will I live ! " (*Conf*. xii. 10).
" Give Thyself unto me, O my God ! Yea, restore
Thyself unto me. Lo, I love Thee ; and if it be
too little, let me love Thee with more might. I
cannot measure my love, that I may know how
much it needs to be enough—that my life may run
to Thy embrace and turn not away, till it be hidden
in the hiding-place of Thy countenance " (xiii. 8).
" Not doubtfully, but with a sure knowledge,
Lord, I love Thee. Thou didst strike my heart
with Thy Word, and I loved Thee ! . . . What
then do I love, when I love Thee ? . . . I love a
certain light, and a certain voice, a certain fragrance,
a certain food, a certain embrace when I love my
God : a light, voice, fragrance, food, embrace of
the inner man. Where that shines upon my soul
which space cannot contain, that sounds which
time cannot sweep away, that is fragrant which is
scattered not by the breeze, that tastes sweet which
when fed upon is not diminished, that clings close
which no satiety disparts. This it is that I love,
when I love my God ! " (x. 6).

Well might the author of such passages say in
one of his letters, " I enjoy at times a vivid realization of things that abide " (*Ep*. iv. 2). In this
little sentence he gives us the key to his conception
of the spiritual life as a growth or pilgrimage
towards the eternal object of love. Our whole
perfection, says Augustine, consists in growing
and not stopping ; it is a steady effort, a march,
voyage, or ascent, but always an ascent of love to

Love—a movement of the changeful creature to "that which abides." Though deeply Christian, there is slight trace in him of the predominantly Christocentric mysticism of St. Paul. The deepest attractions of his soul are towards the Eternal and Unchanging God. "Something not susceptible of change !" is the chilly formula behind which he conceals the rapturous joy of union with Ultimate Reality. Yet of this same "Something" he can exclaim in another mood, "What can I say, my God, my Life, my Holy Joy ? And what can any man say when he speaks of Thee ?" (*Conf.* i. 4). With this deep personal sense of an abiding object of adoration, "fairest yet strongest, near yet far," he has enriched the mystical consciousness of the Church.

Augustine, then, is with St. Paul a source from which all later mystics have drunk deeply and to their profit. Nor is it only on the transcendental side that they are indebted to him. They owe to his influence that virile temper, that insistence on the primary importance of will and desire as the main instruments of our spiritual progress, which give their works such a sane and bracing quality. From him, too, comes their steady recognition of humility and charity as the twin foundations of the true interior life (*Conf.* vii. 20). He was an inspired psychologist, and modern explorations of the soul endorse the accuracy of his statements. "We are nothing else but *wills* . . . love *cannot* be idle . . . love and do what you like ! . . . Virtue is the ordering of love. Perfect love is perfect righteousness. . . . The soul is only perfect in health when it is perfect in love . . . in

Thy Will is our peace . . . my love is my weight." These Augustinian phrases, and many other of his conceptions, reappear in the works of the mediæval school, all of which depend directly upon his teaching.

A third great writer contributed to that complete fusion of Christian and Hellenistic influences which nourished the later mystics of the Church. If through Cassian they received the teaching of the early solitaries on prayer, and Augustine gave them a deeper and richer concept of God's dealings with the soul, it was the mysterious writer known as Dionysius the Areopagite who—going back to Proclus, and through him to Plotinus, for his metaphysical background—brought into Christianity a fresh and awe-struck sense of the unsearchable divine transcendence. Written in Greek toward the end of the fifth century, and probably by a Syrian monk, the Dionysian books became known in the West in the ninth century, when they were translated into Latin by John the Scot. Their influence on the mediæval mystics was great ; and they provided the conceptions by means of which Ruysbroeck and other supreme contemplatives were able to express something of their deepest intuitions of Reality.

In reading Dionysius we must remember that he is struggling by means of an intellectual language borrowed from philosophy—and mainly from Proclus—to describe a non-intellectual and indeed a supra-rational experience : the secret ascent of the soul to God. The Divine Darkness, or Ignorance, of which he speaks is a psychological condition ; in which that soul exchanges discursive

thought for the state of pure fruition, or contemplation, where it achieves " union with Him Who is
above all knowledge and all being."

The great mystics—for whom, no doubt, these
books were chiefly written—have always found in
Dionysius much that explained their loftiest experiences. He lives upon the mountains, and those
who can breathe their rarefied air will understand
his statements ; his perpetual struggle to drive
home the otherness and distinctness of God, the
unspeakable nature even of man's fragmentary
experiences of the Divine. " Our speech is re-
strained in proportion to the height of our ascent ;
but when our ascent is accomplished, speech will
cease altogether and be absorbed into the ineffable."
(*De Myst. Theo.*, cap. iii.)

It is true that the gentleness and intimacy of
Christian feeling are absent ; and no theory of
mysticism based on Dionysius alone could completely represent man's spiritual needs and possibilities. He encourages a dangerous abstraction
from concrete life, and invites unwary spirits to
ascents which few can safely undertake. But he
did great things for the deepening and enrichment
of the mystical consciousness by his emphatic
presentation of the supernatural mystery of the
Divine Nature ; the " Being beyond being,
Existence Uncreate," which enfolds and transcends
all man's partial apprehensions of God. Souls of
many different types have been fed by him : the
unmitigated intellectualism of Eckhart, the passionate fervour of Jacopone da Todi, could find in him
something which tallied with their experience.
Therefore he well completes the trilogy of writers

who developed in this period the growing Christian science of contemplation, and prepared the way for the mysticism of the Mediæval Church.

ILLUSTRATIVE WORKS

Augustine, St.   Confessions : Text and Translation.   (Loeb Classical Library.)   London, 1919.

Bertrand, Louis.   St. Augustine.   London, 1914.

Butler, Dom Cuthbert.   Benedictine Monachism.   London, 1919.

Western Mysticism.   London, 1922.

Cassian, J. Dialogues.   (Select Nicene and Post-Nicene Library.)   Oxford, 1894.

Dionysius the Areopagite.   The Divine Names and Mystical Theology. Trans. C. E. Rolt.   London, 1920.

Hannay, J. O.   The Spirit and Origin of Christian Monasticism.   London, 1903.

Hügel, Baron F. von.   Eternal Life.   London, 1912.

Pourrat, P.   Christian Spirituality.   Vol. i.   London, 1922.

CHAPTER IV

THE EARLY MIDDLE AGES

ST. HILDEGARDE—HELFDE—RICHARD OF ST. VICTOR
—ST. BERNARD

THE centuries following the close of the Patristic period give us the names of few mystics. We need not suppose from this that the mystical life died out, but merely that its experiences were seldom registered. In the eleventh and twelfth centuries, however, a marked revival of mystical religion took place ; and here and there it became articulate, either in the form of a protest against the laxity of the average religious life, or as the effort of those who possessed a first-hand experience of God to communicate their certitude and sense of obligation. Thus St. Peter Damian (1007–72) is chiefly known as a religious reformer, inspired by a more vivid sense of reality than his contemporaries possessed; and the fortunate survival of the Meditations of St. Anselm (1033–1109) reveals the deep reservoirs of mystical devotion, the fervour, humility and love, which fed the active career of that great statesman and ecclesiastic.

In the twelfth century three great names, among many less eminent, express three aspects of the Church's mystical life : the German abbess and prophetess, St. Hildegarde (1098–1179) ; the

Scotch scholar and contemplative, Richard of St. Victor (died about 1173), from whom all the mediæval mystics took their psychology intact ; above all, St. Bernard (1091–1153), a worthy successor of St. Paul and St. Augustine in that line of great constructive mystics to which the Church owes the repeated renewal and development of her inner life.

St. Hildegarde is the first great figure in that line of women mystics—persons of marked intelligence and unquenchable energy—who so completely refute the common accusations brought against mysticism, and so perfectly prove the thesis of St. Teresa that " the object of the spiritual marriage is work."

Of abnormal psychic make-up, weak bodily health, but immense intellectual power, Hildegarde's personality and range of activities would be startling at any period. She founded two convents, wrote a long physical treatise in nine books, including a complete guide to the nature and properties of herbs, was skilled in medicine, deeply interested in politics, sternly denounced ecclesiastical laxity and corruption, and corresponded with and often rebuked the greatest men of her day. She was also a musician and poet, and over sixty hymns are attributed to her. In later life she travelled hundreds of miles in the course of her duties—a considerable matter for an elderly nun of the twelfth century. Yet she remained first and foremost a contemplative, whose actions were always dictated by inward commands, and whose sources of power lay beyond the world.

Thanks to the inquiries of her deeply interested

disciples, and Hildegarde's admirably lucid replies, we know much of her inward experiences. To her, God was Light ; and the light-imagery frequent in the mediæval mystics certainly owes something to her. She gave in old age to the monk Guibert, her secretary and afterwards her biographer, an account of her mystical experience; from which we see that two distinct grades of spiritual apprehension were involved in it. First and rarest, the ecstatic perception of that Living Light which was her name for God—her inspired letters frequently begin "the Living Light saith." Next that diffused radiance which she calls the Shade of the Living Light, and within which her great allegorical visions were seen.

"From my infancy until now, in the 70th year of my age," she says, "my soul has always beheld this Light ; and in it my soul soars to the summit of the firmament and into a different air. . . . The brightness which I see is not limited by space and is more brilliant than the radiance round the sun. . . . I cannot measure its height, length, breadth. Its name, which has been given me, is 'Shade of the Living Light'. . . . Within that brightness I sometimes see another light, for which the name *Lux Vivens* has been given me. When and how I see *this*, I cannot tell ; but sometimes when I see it all sadness and pain is lifted from me, and I seem a simple girl again, and an old woman no more ! "

This quotation alone places Hildegarde among the mystics ; that is to say, those who have experienced an immediate apprehension of God with its gift of freshness and joy. Reading it, we are reminded of Ruysbroeck's utterances concerning the distinction between that Everlasting Light which " is *not* God, but is that light whereby we see Him," and the sudden Light " blazing down as it were a lightning flash from the Face of Divine

Love," bringing "so great a joy and delight of soul and body that a man knoweth not what hath befallen him" (*The XII Béguines*, cap. x). Indeed Hildegarde's works—widely known and much reverenced in succeeding centuries—may have provided the germ of Ruysbroeck's idea.

The "Shade of the Living Light" stands perhaps for that lucid expansion of consciousness in which the seer and the prophet touch fresh levels of knowledge and understanding. Hildegarde, plainly an unusual child, says she first experienced this when only three years old, and at five began to understand the visionary world in which she lived, though a limited vocabulary prevented her from communicating what she saw. During childhood and adolescence she had constant interior visions and premonitions of the future, accompanied by much ill-health. Before dismissing these stories as absurdities we should remember that her career proves her a woman of genius ; and that such spiritual and psychical precocity undoubtedly exists, and is the raw material from which a certain sort of mysticism may develop. A long series of instances, from the call of Samuel to that of Florence Nightingale (visited by an imperative sense of vocation when six years old), warns us that we are far from understanding the conditions underlying human greatness.

Hildegarde's account of her visions is unsensational and exact. They were pictures, she says, seen within the mind, "neither in dream, sleep, nor any frenzy," involving no hallucination and never interfering with her outward sight. "I did not see these things with the bodily eyes or hear them with outward ears, but I beheld them according to God's will, openly and fully awake, considering them in the full light of the mind, eyes and ears of the inner mind. How is this? It is hard for carnal man to understand. . . . When fully penetrated by my light I said many things strange to those who heard them."

She continued frequently and accurately to foresee future events, but only confiding in a few of her fellow-nuns, till the beginning of middle age, when she had been for some years abbess of her convent. Then her real prophetic period opened in a dynamic vision reminiscent of those associated with the calls of the prophets. " In the year 1141 of the Incarnation of the Son of God, at the age of forty-two years seven months, a flaming light of marvellous brightness coming from a rift of heaven, penetrated my brain, heart and breast like a flame that warms but burns not, even as the rays of the sun strike the earth." This light gave her a direct intuition into the spiritual meaning of Scripture, and commanded her to give her revelations to the world. She resisted from motives of humility and reserve, and the resulting conflict brought on a violent illness. Advised to obey her Voice, she began to dictate her revelation, and immediately recovered her health.

For ten years the great symbolic pictures recorded in her book of *Scivias* continued to unroll before her inward eyes, conveying spiritual teaching and prophetic denunciations of the corruptions of the age. She suffered much under the stress of these experiences, spoke often of " this vision which *burns* my soul," and told St. Bernard in late life that since childhood she had never been free from trials. In 1147 another vision revealed the site on which it was ordained that she should build her new convent. She kept this secret, and psychic blindness and lameness at once fell on her. She told her vision, and was healed.

We might hesitate to call St. Hildegarde's outpourings and experiences mystical, were it not for her vivid sense of God and the creative quality of her spiritual life. She initiated a type of mysticism which was continued by her contemporary, the Benedictine Abbess Elizabeth of Schonau (1129–65), and, in the next century, by three nuns of the Convent of Helfde—the fervent and poetic Mechthild of Madgeburg (1210–85), St. Gertrude the Great (1256–1301), and her friend and director, St. Mechthild of Hackeborn (1240–98).

In all these women vivid pictorial visions of Christ and the saints—often directly inspired by the liturgy—or allegorical revelations concerning the mysteries of faith, were the principal media of spiritual apprehension. Thus St. Gertrude's vivid sense of the self-giving love of God found expression in the beautiful symbol of the Sacred Heart. St. Mechthild, whose exquisite voice was one of the glories of Helfde, saw her vocation of praise crystallized in the charming scene in which Christ called her His nightingale. Mechthild of Magdeburg perceived, under romantic imagery which owes much to the secular poetry of the time, the whole course and consummation of the soul's life. The nuns of Helfde lived, we may allow, in a world of imagination; but it was a world in which all the delicate beauties of Nature played a sacramental part, and which was lit by the Divine light. Their glimpses of heaven were full of birds and flowers. Immortal Love came to them, as Mechthild of Magdeburg says, " in the morning dew, in the bird's song." Their own prayers seemed to them like larks, soaring up full of music to God, and hovering before His face. Moreover, a frankly feminine interest in dress and jewellery found innocent satisfaction in many of these visions, with their constant and detailed descriptions of the magnificent robes and symbolic crowns of the saints.

Yet the Church would be the poorer, did an austere and impossible—indeed priggish—demand for " pure reality " insist on the ejection of such visionaries as these from the ranks of the mystics. At their best they are poets and artists of the Ineffable : and, as with other artists, news of a beauty beyond the range of the senses is often given to us through their lovely dreams.

If the current started by St. Hildegarde tended towards a mysticism of a romantic and emotional type, there were sterner elements at work amongst her contemporaries. Equally important for the history of Christian mysticism is the self-effacing personality of the Augustinian Canon Richard of St. Victor (died 1173), the first contemplative to provide a psychological account of mystical states. Richard was a Scotsman, disciple and successor of the philosopher Hugh of St. Victor, a thinker with strong mystical tendencies. Both he and his master were well known in the religious world of the twelfth century, and had intercourse with St. Bernard, though their philosophy does not seem to have influenced him. Richard's life was probably spent chiefly in the Abbey of St. Victor at Paris, and he became Prior of this house some time before his death. Dante's reference to him in the *Paradiso*, as a flaming spirit "who was in contemplation more than man" (*Par.* x, 132), proves that he was regarded by mediæval theologians as a great practical mystic; indeed, we recognize behind his impersonal utterances the note of personal ardour and certitude. His influence on later mystics was immense and beneficent, and the mystical theology of a Church which has now almost forgotten his existence remains deeply in his debt.

Richard, though he regarded merely secular learning with suspicion, and described it as "tasteless wisdom," was a person of great intellectual power. He definitely connected mystical with mental activity. By reason, he said, we can contemplate visible and comprehensible things; and thence the mind of the contemplative ascends, in an orderly manner, to the beholding of invisible things beyond the reach of reason. In this mystical apprehension he discovered three stages: first, the dilation of the mind, which thus realizes its own capacity for a wider and more wonderful span of experience; then that uplifting of the mind into things above itself which is the essence of prayer; and finally that snatching away or utter "alienation" of the mind to another sphere of reality, which constitutes ecstasy.

This doctrine is developed in three works: *Benjamin Minor, or the Preparation of the Soul; Benjamin Major, or Contemplation;* and the lovely little tract on the *Four Degrees of Burning Love,* which exhibits the perfecting of the soul as a parallel growth in love and prayer. The first stage is nourished by meditation : he compares it to betrothal. The second degree is the " wedding," which binds the human to the Divine spirit, and is expressed in the deep intercourse of the " prayer of quiet." The third degree involves that complete surrender or self-merging in which, as he mysteriously says, " the soul no longer thirsts *for* God, but *into* God," and its prayer is, or may be, ecstasy. The final degree is a divine creativeness, the " transforming union," in which " the soul brings forth its children," and which is the real object of all that has gone before. In this doctrine Richard gives us a key to the lives of the great mystics, and demolishes any conception of mysticism centred on the soul's mere enjoyment of God. All the great figures of Christian sanctity—Paul, Augustine, Bernard, Francis, Teresa—are in their last and life-giving stages triumphant examples of Richard's " divine fecundity."

He made other gifts of great value to the developing science of the spiritual life. He pointed to a rigorous self-knowledge as an important part of purification ; meaning by this knowledge not only of our sins, but of our possibilities. Such self-knowledge he compares with a high mountain, climbed with much effort. When we reach the top we discover a horizon so great that we realize our own littleness. Yet this discovery of ourselves in the atmosphere of reality is not to be confused with true contemplation : for though such discreet effort, devotion, and wonder all predispose the soul for the mystical experience, they will never produce it. That experience is, as later writers said, given or " infused." Richard was perhaps the first to lay down this distinction between natural and supernatural prayer. As we might expect in an Augustinian canon, after the Bible his chief source is St. Augustine, whose tradition of the spiritual life he carries on. We cannot read the mystics of the Middle Ages, especially of the English school, without realizing how great was his influence : how fully, in spite of the humble suppression of his own experiences, he conformed to the demands of " divine fecundity."

The effect of the Victorine teaching, however, was surpassed by that of St. Bernard, the dominant figure in twelfth-century religious life. Born in 1090, and entering the newly-formed Cistercian order at the age of twenty-two, Bernard's greatness was so quickly perceptible that three years later he was sent to found the monastery of Clairvaux, remaining its abbot till his death in 1153. He thus doubled the careers of monastic founder and spiritual teacher, also exercising much influence on contemporary politics.

The early history of the Cistercian abbeys of Great Britain shows us the austerity, industry, and charity which formed part of St. Bernard's ideal, and with which he inspired his sons. His personal attractiveness and shining example drew hundreds of novices, including his parents and all his brothers, to the religious life ; and at his death the Cistercian order—barely existent when he entered it—possessed 350 abbeys and 150 dependent cells.

The life of this great creative spirit was one of ceaseless activities, many journeys, much administrative work. He rebuked the Papacy and preached a Crusade. Yet he retained the simplicity and radiant charm which are the prerogatives of those who share St. Catherine of Siena's power of "making a little cell in the heart." The chance words of a visitor to Clairvaux give us in a phrase the real Bernard, warmed by a secret flame ; and explain his gift for making and keeping devoted friends. St. Bernard's own cell, said this observer, was more fit for a leper than for an abbot : nevertheless " he welcomed us joyously. We asked how he fared ; and he smiled at us in that generous way of his, and said ' Splendidly ! ' " [1] Thanks to this real, but not rigid, love of poverty, solitude and lowliness, he remained a pure contemplative ; and was fitly chosen by Dante as the initiator of the soul into the highest secrets of Paradise :

> Quale è colui, che forse di Croazia
>   viene a veder la Veronica nostra,
>   che per l'antica fama non si sazia,
> Ma dice nel pensier, fin che si mostra :
> Signor mio Gesù Cristo, Dio verace,
>   or fu sì fatta la sembianza vostra ?
> Tale era io mirando la vivace
>   carità di colui, che in questo mondo
>   contemplando gustò di quella pace.[2]

Bernard's love was of that living and generous sort which marks the creative mystic. He says

---

[1] Given by Coulton, *Five Centuries of Religion*, p. 321.

[2] As is he, who perhaps from Croatia comes to behold our Veronica, who because of its ancient fame is not sated, but says in thought, so long as it is shown " My Lord Jesu Christ, true God, and was Thy countenance thus made ? " Such was I, gazing upon the living love of him, who in this world by contemplation tasted of that peace. (*Par.* xxxi. 103–11.)

that he who loves indeed will desire, beyond vision, the penetration of God into the very ground of the heart; and the earnest of this experience is to be its practical effect. Like Richard of St. Victor, he held that union with God must issue in creativeness. " Souls like holy mothers may bring forth souls by their labours, or by their meditations may give birth to spiritual truths." Moreover, he practised what he preached. Though a life of silence and prayer was doubtless what he loved, he never shirked the active side of existence, or failed to act up to his own declaration that the whole object of contemplation was to make men better shepherds of souls. We may be sure that he is speaking from personal experience when he says, in the forty-first sermon on the Canticles, that "Often enough we ask for one thing and get another—long for the repose of contemplation and are given the laborious office of preaching—long for the Bridegroom's presence, and are given the task of bringing forth and nourishing His children instead . . . the embrace of divine contemplation must often be interrupted in order to give nourishment to the little ones, and none may live for himself alone, but for all " (*Cant.*, 41).

St. Bernard's mystical teaching is chiefly found in the little treatise on the *Love of God*—written when he was thirty-five years of age, and before the most strenuous period of his active life—and in the series of eighty-six sermons on the Canticles, preached to his monks at Clairvaux. In these, the whole course and character of a spiritual life and the love that informs it are analysed and described, with marvellous eloquence and surety of touch, with special reference to the symbolism of the Song of Solomon.

Imagery of this kind is apt to displease modern readers, who seldom possess the shining purity of soul which safeguarded those who first employed it. But his metaphors cannot obscure the simplicity, sanity and depth of Bernard's mysticism; which continues Cassian's solid doctrine of a deepening communion with Spirit, reached through self-discipline and the degrees of prayer. Bernard, towards the end of his life, tried, with the candour of the truly humble, to tell his own experience of this :

Bear with my foolishness for a little, for I want to tell you, as I promised, how these things took place in me. This is indeed of no importance; I put myself forward only in order to be useful to you, and if you are helped I am consoled for my egoism; if not, I shall have exhibited my folly. I confess, then, to speak foolishly, that the Word has visited me—indeed, very often. But, though He has frequently come into my soul, I have never at any time been aware of the moment of His coming. I have felt Him present, I remember He has been with me, I have sometimes even had a premonition of His coming, but never have I felt His coming or departure. . . . It is not by the eyes that He enters, for He has no colour; nor by the ears, for His coming is silent; nor by the nostrils, for He is blended with the mind, and not with the air; nor again does He enter by the mouth, for His nature cannot be eaten or drunk; nor lastly can we trace Him by touch, for He is intangible. You will ask then how, since His track is thus traceless, I could know that He is present? Because He is living and full of energy, and as soon as He has entered me, has quickened my sleeping soul, and aroused, softened and goaded my heart, which was torpid and hard as a stone. He has begun to pluck up and destroy, plant and build, to water the dry places, light up the dark places, throw open what was shut, inflame with warmth what was cold, straighten the crooked path and make rough places smooth. . . . In the reformation and renewal of the spirit of my mind, that is my inward man, I have seen something of the loveliness of His Beauty, and meditating on these things have been filled with wonder at the multitude of His greatness. But when the Word withdrew, all these spiritual powers and faculties began to droop and languish, as if the fire were taken from beneath a bubbling pot; and this is to me the sign of His departure. Then my soul must needs be sad and sorry, till He comes back and my heart again warms within me as it is wont; for this is to me the sign that He has returned. (*Cant.*, 74, condensed.)

Such a mysticism represents, not so much an experience of transcendent Reality, as communion with the soul's Strengthener and Friend ; and was perhaps the characteristic form taken by St. Bernard's developed spirituality, compensating and supporting the ceaseless activities of his later life. He was well aware of its incompleteness, the extent to which it was limited by the human instrument : " So long as this poor wall of the body endures," he says, " that ray of utmost brightness comes not in through open doors, but only through narrow slits "—a phrase which brings to mind the loopholes through which shafts of vivid sunlight from the outer world entered the gloomy castles of the twelfth century. But his rich consciousness of God could also express itself through another and more transcendental type of contemplation, characteristic perhaps of his earlier and more leisured years—that " Fourth Degree of Love " in which the soul in utter self-forgetfulness seems merged in God, " suddenly, and for the space of hardly a moment " (*The Love of God*, cap. x). Such capacity to " lose thyself as though thou wert not, and to be utterly unconscious of thyself and to be emptied of thyself " (*ibid.*) is, he says " altogether divine and utterly unintelligible save to those who have experienced it. . . . Then the soul, transported out of herself, is granted a clearer vision of the Divine Majesty, yet only for a moment and with the swiftness of a lightning flash " (*Cant.*, 41).

The influence of St. Bernard's writings on the mystics of the later Middle Ages was great. They constantly quote him and appeal to his authority ; and beyond this, their unacknowledged debts are considerable. Indeed, it is scarcely excessive to say that his teaching coloured the whole spiritual life of the mediæval Church. That beautiful cult of the Holy Name, which became prominent in English mysticism, finds its literary source in his fifteenth sermon on the Canticles. Reading it, we can hardly resist the conclusion that this sermon inspired at least the opening stanzas of the hymn *Jesu dulcis memoria*—once, though no longer, attributed to Bernard himself—which so decisively influenced mediæval spirituality; providing a mould, at once intimate and poetic, into which its ardent Christocentric feeling could flow. As with St. Augustine, so here, many thoughts and images with which later mystics are credited have a Bernardine source. Thus even Pascal's most celebrated saying—" In that thou hast sought Me, thou hast already found Me," repeats a phrase in Bernard's *Love of God*—" Herein is a wondrous thing ! None can seek Thee save whoso first has found ! " and doubtless by far the largest number of such borrowings are still untraced. He was one of those creative spirits on whom succeeding generations feed : whose experience is not for themselves alone, but enriches the whole life of the Church.

ILLUSTRATIVE WORKS

Bernard, St. Sermons on the Canticles. 2 vols. Dublin, 1920.

The Love of God. Translated by Edmund Gardner. London, 1916.

Butler, Dom Cuthbert. Western Mysticism. London, 1922.

Coulton, G. G. Five Centuries of Religion. Cambridge, 1923.

Gertrude, St. Prayers of St. Gertrude and St. Mechthilde. Translated by Rev. T. Alder Pope. London, 1917.

Hildegarde, St. Vie. Paris, 1907.

Révelations. 2 vols. Paris, 1912.

Mechthild, St. (of Hackeborn). Révelations. Paris, 1919.

Morison, J. Cotter. Life and Times of St. Bernard. London, 1868.

Pourrat, P. Christian Spirituality. Vol. ii. London, 1923.

Taylor, H. O. The Mediæval Mind. London, 1914.

CHAPTER V

FRANCISCAN MYSTICISM

ST. FRANCIS—THE SPIRITUAL FRANCISCANS— JACOPONE DA TODI—ANGELA OF FOLIGNO

WITH the career of St. Francis of Assisi (1182–1226) something new entered the spiritual life of the Church. He emerged from the " rut of use and wont," to make a fresh contact with reality ; and this contact took the form of a mysticism which was penitential, uncloistered, poetic and Christlike. Since in varying degrees and ways these qualities reappeared in the spiritual experience of his followers, enriching through them the Christian consciousness, Francis must rank with those creative personalities to whom all the deepest developments of this consciousness are due.

As St. Francis is of all the mediæval saints the one who is most familiar and beloved, it is needless to tell again the story of his life. But regarded in its mystical aspect—that is, as an ever-deepening capacity for the experience of God—the emphasis of that life does not always fall upon the episodes for which he is now most commonly admired. He was, above all else, a spiritual realist, who wished his inward and his outward life to be at one : we shall never learn to know him by studying or admiring his outward actions, unless we perceive these as the expressions of an unwavering interior attitude. We may prefer to call him a " little brother of the birds," forgetting that he was also a " little brother of the lice " ; we shall only understand and correlate these facts when we remember that he first called himself and his companions the " penitents of Assisi." He accepted in the most practical sense the old ascetic prescription of an unmitigated meekness and an unlimited love, as the double foundations of all true relationship between created and uncreated Spirit. The story which represents him as repeating throughout a night of prayer the single awestruck aspiration : " My God ! my God ! what art Thou ? and what am I ? ", though its form may be legendary, fulfils the real office of legend in preserving a truth for which external history finds no room. It hints at the greatness and the depth of Francis's soul, the humility and sense of mystery, the ceaseless craving for the Infinite, which underlay his gaiety and charm ; and is a useful corrective to the more amiable and ordinary view of his character as a " Bridegroom of Lady Poverty " and " Troubadour of Christ."

Again, the object of that external poverty on which he laid such stress was transcendental : for him it was a means, not the end it became for his more fanatical adherents. He is credited with calling it " the heavenly virtue whereby all earthly things and fleeting are trodden under foot and all hindrances lifted from the soul, so that she may be free to unite herself to the Eternal God " (*Fioretti*, cap. xiii)—thus emphasizing the true aim and interest of his life, and refusing to countenance anything that conflicted with it. In other words, he hated property, not because it was a source of sin, but because it split an attention which should be devoted to the one object of worship and love, and turned the relation of brotherhood within which all living things should adore their common Father into a relation of ownership. Many have seen this truth, at least intermittently ; the distinction of St. Francis is that he insisted upon acting on it. Thus his great follower, Jacopone da Todi, condensed the Franciscan method and secret in a phrase when he wrote :

> Povertate è nulla avere
> e nulla cosa poi volere ;
> ed omne cosa possedere
> en spirito de libertate.

(Poverty is naught to have, and nothing to desire ; and all things to possess in the spirit of liberty.) (*Lauda* 60.)

From his conversion onwards, the whole outward career of Francis was a dramatic explication of this principle : and the result was a life, and relationship with Reality, quickly recognized by his followers as Christlike in a unique degree. A real return to the Gospels is always startling, whatever the circumstances in which it takes place. The return made by St. Francis seemed to his contemporaries so amazing in its novelty, vigour and completeness, and in the transformation it effected, that he came to be regarded by his disciples and their immediate successors as, above all, the perfect imitator of Christ : one, indeed, in whom the actual earthly life of Jesus was reproduced. " Christ hath shown Himself in thee ! " said Jacopone da Todi with his usual boldness.

FRANCISCAN MYSTICISM

More attractive is the form taken by this conception in the beautiful mind of Pier Pettignano (*ob*. 1289), that humble Franciscan contemplative whom all readers of Dante love. He saw in vision a superb procession of Apostles, Saints and Martyrs, with the Blessed Virgin at their head ; all walking carefully and scrutinizing the ground with much earnestness, that they might tread as nearly as possible in the very footsteps of Christ. At the end of this pageant of the Church Triumphant came the little shabby figure of Francis, barefoot and brown-robed ; and he alone was walking easily and steadily in the actual footprints of our Lord. Such tales as these show what the life and rule of Francis meant to those who were touched by his spirit ; and give the starting-point of Franciscan mysticism, with its love of poverty and vivid Christocentric feeling.

The peculiar concentration on the Passion which unites all the Franciscan mystics, of course results from the episode of the Stigmata, which deeply impressed the mediæval religious mind. Whatever be our opinion of this episode, it witnesses to the intense and mystical character of that inner life which St. Francis—like his Pattern—so well concealed from the outer world. As the Gospels tell almost nothing about the interior education that ended in Gethsemane ; so the gradual development of the spirit of Francis during the eighteen years of his religious life can only be judged by its culmination on La Verna, when, for an instant, the body became completely docile to the longings and apprehensions of the soul.

All the great Franciscan mystics, differing widely

in temperament from each other and from Francis himself, live under the spell of this event. It gives them the passionate enthusiasm for suffering on the one hand, the rapturous and almost lyrical joy in surrender on the other, with which they enriched the consciousness of the Church. This ecstasy of self-giving, this paradoxical union of painful and delighted love, is not, of course, chiefly to be sought within the respectable ranks of those " conventual " friars who learnt so soon to interpret the Rule of Poverty in accordance with comfort and common sense. It was preserved and handed on by the saintly brothers who kept intact the spirit of St. Francis ; men living chiefly in remote hermitages, where they observed the Primitive Rule in all its rigour and passed their time in prayer. We know that Brother Leo, the intimate friend of Francis, was living thus in his old age. So, too, were his friend Conrad of Offida (1241–1306), who had inherited the Franciscan power over animals, and into whom the very soul of the mystical Brother Giles was said to have passed ; and the holy ecstatic John of La Verna, whose " heart for full three years was kindled with the fire of Love Divine " so that " his marvellous and celestial words changed the hearts of men." John of La Verna was Jacopone da Todi's friend and probable director in the spiritual life, and it is likely enough that his beautiful spirit inspired some at least of his pupil's poems. Besides these, we may be sure that a number of inarticulate mystics were among those friars of the Spiritual Party in whom it was said that " Christ and His Spirit were most firmly believed to dwell."

FRANCISCAN MYSTICISM

These humble servants of the supernatural were known, revered, and visited in their retreats by all who valued the life of the Spirit ; and thus preserved and disseminated in its ardour and purity the inner character of Franciscan mysticism.

Second only to their influence was the part played by the Franciscan Tertiaries. These were men and women of all ranks, living in the world, who were drawn by the unmatched attraction of the Franciscan appeal and demand to accept such a modified rule of simplicity and devotion as was consistent with ordinary life ; and formed a loosely-knit society devoted to spiritual religion. It was within this society that the great Franciscan mystics —Pier Pettignano, Jacopone da Todi, Angela of Foligno, and Ubertino da Casale—developed : and we misunderstand their position if we look at them in isolation, forgetting their dependence on environment. When Jacopone wrote his spiritual songs there were already in the chief Italian cities sympathetic groups waiting to receive and sing them. It was to members of such groups that Angela of Foligno addressed her *Instructions*. The lofty nature of the doctrine contained in her letters and exhortations to her " spiritual sons " shows their degree of spiritual understanding ; and suggests that Ubertino da Casale had more than their voluntary poverty in mind when he called these Tertiaries " great practisers of seraphic wisdom." From two of them, an unknown mystic called Cecilia of Florence and the holy Pier Pettignano of Siena, he says that he first learnt " the whole art of the higher contemplation of the Life of Christ " ; and that " it would be a wondrous thing if the clearness of their spirit could be set down in words." Putting such a statement beside the poems of Jacopone, we begin to realize the existence in the thirteenth-century Italy of a widespread society of Franciscan mystics, not only rapt contemplatives, but also eager missionaries and teachers ; persons whose enthusiasm and love " set other loving spirits on fire." Those whom we know were nearly always, like Francis, " twice-born " souls : vigorous men and women, full of passionate feeling or ambition, captured, converted, and turning all their energy towards spiritual aims. Thus Jacopone da Todi was an ambitious lawyer who was converted in middle life, according to the legend, by a crushing sorrow. It is said that the sudden death of his beautiful young wife, and the discovery that under her lovely clothes she wore the hair shirt of the penitent, drove him to embrace Franciscan poverty and abjection in its most drastic sense. He became in turn a wandering missionary, a poet, a leader among the Spiritual Franciscans, and finally a great contemplative. His poems, revealing his passage through all the phases of penitence, rapture, desolation and peaceful assurance which mark mystical growth are the perfect literary monument of Franciscan spirituality ; its intensity of emotion, its religious realism, its paradoxical combination of austere penitence and gentle sweetness, its sudden flights into the unseen.

> 'Nante che el provasse, demandava
> amare Cristo, credendo dolzura ;
> en pace de dolceza star pensava,
> for d'ogni pena possedendo altura ;
> pruovo tormento qual non me cuitava,
> che'l cor se me fendesse per calura ;

non posso dar figura
de que veggio sembianza,
che moio en delettanza
e vivo senza core.

*   *   *   *

Gia non posso vedere creatura,
al Creatore grida tutta mente ;
cielo né terra non me dá dolzura,
per Cristo amore tutto m'è fetente ;
luce de sole sí me pare oscura,
vedendo quella faccia resplendente,
cherubin son niente,
belli per ensegnare,
serafin per amare,
chi vede lo Signore.

Before I knew its power, I asked in prayer
  For love of Christ, believing it was sweet ;
I thought to breathe a calm and tranquil air,
  On peaceful heights where tempests never beat.
Torment I find instead of sweetness there.
  My heart is riven by the dreadful heat ;
  Of these strange things to treat
    All words are vain ;
    By bliss I am slain,
    And yet I live and move.

*   *   *   *

Now on no creature can I turn my sight ;
  But on my Maker all my mind is set.
Earth, sea, and sky are emptied of delight,
  For Christ's dear love all else I clean forget :
All else seems vile, day seems as dark as night ;
  Cherubim, seraphim, in whom are met
  Wisdom and Love, must yet
    Give place, give place,
    To that one Face
    To my dear Lord of Love.
                (*Lauda* 90.) [1]

---

[1] This and the following quotations from Jacopone are taken by kind permission from the translation of Mrs. Theodore Beck.

In this magnificent poem, rising to an almost intolerable pitch of emotion, we see Franciscan enthusiasm at fever-heat ; needing and receiving the stern reminder—placed by the poet on the lips of Christ, but really taken direct from St. Augustine—that all virtue consists in the right ordering of love.

> Ordena questo amore, tu che m'ami,
> non è virtute senza ordene trovata,
> poiché trovare tanto tu m'abrami,
> ca mente con virtute è renovata
> a me amare, voglio che tu chiami
> la caritate qual sia ordenata.

Order this love, O thou who lovest Me,
  For without order virtue comes to naught ;
And since thou seekest Me so ardently—
  That virtue may be ruler in thy thought
And in thy love—summon that Charity
  Whose fervours are by gentle order taught.

(*Lauda* 90.)

But other, gentler, and indeed loftier moods are celebrated in Jacopone's verse—verse which, with all its insistence on the merits of poverty and simplicity, its implied contempt for scholarship, clearly reveals the literary sources of all the poet's most striking phrases and ideas. Whilst direct Franciscan influence accounts for the hymns to Holy Poverty and to St. Francis, the lovely Christmas carols, the poems on the Cross, others show considerable knowledge of mystical philosophy. St. Augustine and Dionysius the Areopagite were obviously familiar to him, and constantly furnish his most striking phrases ; and from these great masters, with their Platonic outlook, he learnt to suggest, almost to describe, that ecstatic sense of the Being of God—that transcendental background to the soul's life, and object of its adoration—which balances and enfolds all personal strivings and desires.

Se l'atto de la mente
è tutto consopito,
en Dio stando rapito,
ch'en sé non se retrova,
de sé reman perdente
posto nello 'nfinito,
ammira co c'è gito,
non sa como se mova.
Tutto sí se renova,
tratto fuor de suo stato,
en quello smesurato
dove s'anega l'amore.

When the mind's very being is gone,
    Sunk in a conscious sleep,
In a rapture divine and deep,
    Itself in the Godhead lost :
It is conquered, ravished, and won !
    Set in Eternity's sweep,
    Gazing back on the steep,
Knowing not how it was crossed—
To a new world now it is tossed,
    Drawn from its former state,
    To another, measureless, great,
    Where Love is drowned in the Sea.
                                        (*Lauda* 91.)

This two-fold outlook towards both the personal-emotional and the impersonal-metaphysical experience of God—a duality pushed by Jacopone to its extreme point—is found again in Angela of Foligno, his junior by about twenty years, and in many respects the most remarkable of the great Franciscan mystics. The redeeming character of Franciscan enthusiasm—its ability to change, brace, and expand the most unlikely spirits and impel them to exacting discipline and selfless work—are fully shown in her.

Angela is an admirable example of that which the Abbé Huvelin was accustomed to call a " bit by bit spirituality." Even allowing for the exaggeration of the penitent, she had clearly lived, until the beginning of middle age, a thoroughly worldly and even a sinful life ; yet she became one of the great religious influences of her day, and was called, not without reason, a " Mistress in Theology." Her best known disciple, Ubertino da Casale, has left an impressive picture of her spiritual power ; and that which he experienced we may be sure that many others experienced too.

Ubertino was a vain, brilliant and self-indulgent young friar, whose first initiation into the spiritual life, at the hands of Cecilia of Florence and Pier Pettignano, had merely stimulated his religious imagination and stopped short of real self-renouncement. He preached brilliantly but lived comfortably ; and his complete conversion was only effected when he came under the influence of Angela at about forty years of age, and received through her direction the strength of purpose he required.

She restored, even a thousand-fold, all the gifts of my soul that I had lost through my sinfulness, so that from henceforth I was not the same man as before. When I had experienced the splendour of her ardent virtue, she changed the whole face of my mind ; and so drove out weakness and languor from my soul and body, and renewed my mind that was torn asunder with distractions, that no one who had known me before could doubt that the spirit of Christ was begotten anew within me through her. (*Arbor Vitæ*, Prologue.)

FRANCISCAN MYSTICISM

The woman of whom this was written, at that time about fifty years old, had passed through a long apprenticeship and much interior suffering before reaching the creative levels of spiritual life.

She had, like most of the great mystics, strong natural passions, and endured prolonged struggle in the course of their sublimation and dedication to spiritual ends. A married woman in prosperous circumstances, she loved human life, with its luxuries and comforts ; was sensual, self-indulgent, vacillating and insincere ; and first combined full enjoyment of the world with the pretended practice of Franciscan austerity.

Being the while full of greediness, gluttony and drunkenness, I feigned to desire naught, save what was needful. I diligently made an outward show of being poor, but caused many sheets and coverings to be put where I lay down to sleep, and to be taken up in the morning so that none might see them. . . . I was given over to pride and the devil, but I feigned to have God in my soul and His consolation in my chamber, whereas I had the devil alike in my soul and my chamber. And know, that during the whole of my life, I have studied how I might obtain the fame of sanctity. (*Book of Conversion*, cap. i.)

This picture is not attractive ; seldom, indeed, has more unpromising material been used for the making of a saint.

Angela was probably at this time a nominal Franciscan Tertiary, evading the real obligations of the rule. Furthermore she had committed grave sins which she was afraid to confess, until, praying to St. Francis, he appeared to her in a dream, and promised her help. Going next day to the cathedral of Foligno, she saw in its pulpit her uncle Arnaldo, a Franciscan friar, and recognizing in him the promised helper, made her confession to him—thus taking the first of the " spiritual steps " by which she " came to know the imperfections of her life," and sought to correct them.

This process lasted for years. There were often long pauses before the next step was seen, the next renunciation faced. It began by a reduction in the comforts of life, " a shameful and a hard thing to do, seeing that I did not feel much love for God, and was living with my husband." A more thoroughgoing asceticism became possible with Angela's widowhood, especially as her children died about this time—perhaps of one of the epidemics which periodically swept the Umbrian towns—and also her mother, " a great hindrance to me in following the way of God." Living with one companion as a Franciscan Tertiary, she now gradually gave up her possessions, the interior call to the complete practice of Franciscan poverty struggling with her natural fear of hardship. She undertook secret penances, and penetrated more deeply into the contemplative life.

She gives a very human account of her hesitation before this total and heroic renunciation of pro-perty. " I cherished," she says, " in imagination a great desire to become poor, and such was my zeal that I often feared to die before attaining the state of poverty. On the other hand I was assailed by temptations, whispering that I was young, and that begging for alms might lead into great danger and shame ; and if I did it, I should be obliged to die in hunger, cold and nakedness. Moreover all my friends dissuaded me from it." These prudent advisers seem even to have included the

Franciscan friars from whom she sought counsel ; but an impulse stronger than all prudence warned her that no half-measures would suffice. " Methought I could not keep *anything* for myself, without greatly offending Him who did thus enlighten me."

It was when she decided upon full renunciation of property that Angela first knew the joys as well as the compulsions of the spiritual life. Hitherto she had been " sunk in bitterness because of her sins, and feeling no divine sweetness whatsoever." But after she had resolved on perfect poverty, she was given " so clear an understanding of the Divine goodness and mine own unworthiness that I could in no way describe it," and from this time began to " feel the sweetness and consolation of God in her heart."

The state of illumination was completed and her consecration assured by the most celebrated of her spiritual "revelations"; the experience which befell her as she went on a pilgrimage from Foligno to Assisi. She tells us that a little time before, whilst she was still distributing the remainder of her property to the poor, she had said to God in prayer, " Lord, that which I do, I do only that I may find Thee," and it seemed to her that a voice replied, " Strive diligently to make thyself ready, for when thou hast accomplished that which thou art now doing, the whole Trinity will descend unto thee." The most ancient MS. of Angela's revelations tells us that it was precisely when she came to the little chapel of the Holy Trinity, where the road from Spello turns towards Assisi, that she suddenly felt her soul inundated by the Presence of God, who spoke to her and " persuaded her to love," promising to remain with her till her second visit to the basilica of Assisi.

It is a mark of Angela's strength of soul, that she did not accept even this overwhelming experience without criticism. " My soul said further : If Thou who hast spoken with me from the beginning wert truly the Holy Spirit, Thou wouldst not have told me such great things ; and if Thou wert verily within me, then my joy would be so great that I could not bear it and live." The inner Presence replied : " I will give thee this sign, that thou mayest know who I am. Go now, and endeavour to speak with thy companions and think of anything thou willst, good or evil, and thou shalt see thou canst not think of aught save God ; for I am He who alone can bind the thoughts."

The experience remained with her until the pilgrims paid their second visit to the basilica, and then " departed with great gentleness ; not suddenly, but slowly and gradually." Nevertheless the sense of abandonment was so bitter that she fell upon the ground ; struggling to say " Love ! love ! why do you leave me ? Why ? Why ? " but able only to utter loud inarticulate cries. The friars ran to see the cause of this uproar, and among them Arnaldo, annoyed that his niece should create a disturbance. When they met next in Foligno, he examined her as to the cause of her seizure ; and under pressure she revealed the unsuspected facts of her mystical life, and the height of contemplative experience which—apparently without formal training of any kind—she had achieved. Arnaldo wrote at her dictation the unequalled series of "intellectual visions" which give her a special place among the mystics of the Church. Their association lasted from the time of the pilgrimage to Assisi until some date subsequent to 1296. We possess the results of Arnaldo's efforts, edited and rearranged by a later hand; and though Angela frequently complained of their inadequacy, insisting that his words were "dry and savourless" and hardly suggested the ineffable truths which were revealed to her, this record remains one of the greatest monuments of Christian mysticism.

The eyes of my soul were opened, and I beheld the plenitude of God, whereby I did comprehend the whole world, both here and beyond the sea, and the abyss and all things else; and therein did I behold naught save the divine power in a manner assuredly indescribable, so that through excess of marvelling the soul cried with a loud voice, saying, "This whole world is full of God!" Wherefore did I now comprehend that the world is but a small thing; I saw, moreover, that the power of God was above all things, and that the whole world was filled with it.

Then said He unto me, "I have shown thee something of My power," the which I did so well understand that it enabled me better to understand all other things. He said also, "I have made thee to see something of My power; behold now and see My humility." Then was I given so deep an insight into the humility of God towards man and all other things, that when my soul remembered His unspeakable power and comprehended His deep humility, it marvelled greatly and did esteem itself to be nothing at all, for in itself it beheld nothing save pride.

Even in the fragmentary form in which we possess it, such a "vision" as this, half-metaphysical and half-personal, in which "the soul beholds a spiritual and not a bodily presence," helps us to understand how Angela came to be called a "Mistress in

Theology "—one who saw deeply into the mysteries of the supernatural world. In them, as in some of the revelations of Julian of Norwich, a direct and supra-rational intuition seems to fuse with the brooding thought of an intensely religious mind. These visions began early and seem to have characterized her first or ecstatic period of development, which ended in 1294, " the year of the pontificate of Celestino "—one of few fixed dates which we possess for her life. They probably correspond with the spiritual stages she calls " unction, instruction, reformation and union."

She was now living in great retirement, her mystical experiences unknown except to her companion and her director, as St. Teresa lived during the first or ecstatic period of her spiritual life. This phase of development, in which she says that sometimes she was so inundated with spiritual joy that her " face was shining and rosy, and her eyes shone like candles," closed in 1294, when she entered the " degree of torments " ; that state of misery which so often precedes the creative stage of the mystic way. Its afflictions lasted for over two years, the trials through which she passed leaving her body " weak, feeble, and full of pain." Violent temptations tested and braced her will. Of the final stages of purification she says : " Every vice was reawakened within me . . . at times, I was thrown into a most horrible darkness of spirit. . . . Methought I would have chosen rather to be roasted than to endure such pains." Those who find in such confessions evidence of a morbid and unbalanced mind must remember that this drastic education formed no mere hysterical vision-

ary, but the woman of genius round whom there
presently gathered a devoted band of disciples,
whose " Evangelical Doctrine " taught many of
the saints, whose meditations on the Divine Attri-
butes still command our astonished respect, and
whose " ardent virtue " changed the whole spiritual
outlook of Ubertino da Casale and shamed him
into complete self-consecration. When he visited
her in 1298, the converted worldling and secret
visionary had become so great a centre of spiritual
influence that Ubertino was not afraid to call her,
in the words of Ecclesiasticus, " the Mother of fair
love and fear and knowledge and holy hope."
The degree of " torment " was passed, and succeeded by that active yet peaceful abiding in God
which she calls " ineffable " and other mystics
name the " unitive life." During this apostolic
period most of her recorded visions concern the
" spiritual sons " who had now become her main
interest. The little book of " Evangelical Doctrine,"
which shows her to us as a teacher and director
of souls, appears to be made of letters and dis-
courses addressed to them in the last ten or
twelve years of her life ; and represents far better
than " visions," " consolations," or " elevations "
can do the proper fruits of spiritual maturity.
Here we see her in her creative aspect, as a
sober instructress in the plain ways which lead to
perfection.

For Angela, the beginning and end of true
wisdom was " to know God and ourselves "—a
level of reality which few human beings achieve.
" Oh, my beloved sons ! every vision, every revelation, all sweetness and emotion, all knowledge,

all contemplation, availeth nothing if a man know not God and himself ! " This realistic knowledge, this sense of spiritual proportion, depends on the soul's humility and poverty. In true Franciscan fashion, she identifies this lowliness and emptiness of spirit with that literal imitation of the earthly life of Christ to which every awakened soul is bound. " The love of God," she observes in a celebrated passage, " is never idle, for it constrains us to follow the way of the Cross ! " This active love is awakened by an attention to God " constant, assiduous, devout, and ardent "—a string of adjectives which suggests the completeness of spiritual life she required of her " sons." It means long and serious training in character-building, prayer and contemplation ; not an emotional piety of the revivalistic type. This training assumes both the existence and the attainableness of supernatural truth. " The first step to be taken by the soul who enters upon this strait way, and desires to draw near to God, is to learn to know God in very truth, and not only outwardly as though by the colour of the writing. For as we know, so do we love ; therefore if we know but little and darkly, if we reflect and meditate on Him only superficially and fleetingly, we shall in consequence love Him but little." Real love is to be directed with discretion, and shown in the acceptance of hardship and contempt, the practice of humility, gentleness, and steadfastness—a catalogue of virtues which perhaps reflects the course followed by Angela's own interior transformation. And the end of this hard process is declared to be the revelation that " *all* goodness cometh from the Love

FRANCISCAN MYSTICISM

Uncreate, and not from ourselves—whosoever feeleth this hath the Spirit of Truth ! "

" Thou," said Jacopone da Todi more tersely, " art the Love wherewith the heart loves Thee." In these two sayings, so deceptive in their simplicity, so infinite in their scope, we reach the heart of Franciscan mysticism.

ILLUSTRATIVE WORKS

Angela of Foligno. Book of Divine Consolations. (New Mediæval Library.) London, 1908.

Cuthbert, Fr. Life of St. Francis of Assisi. London, 1914.

Dante. Divine Comedy : Text and Translation. 3 vols. (Temple Classics.) London, 1900.

Gardner, Edmund. Dante and the Mystics. London, 1913.

Gebhart, E. Mystics and Heretics in Italy. London, 1922.

Jacopone da Todi. Le Laude. A Cura di G. Ferri. Bari. 1915.

Little Flowers of St. Francis. Translated by T. W. Arnold. London, 1903.

Mirror of Perfection. Translated by R. Steele. London, 1903

Sacrum Commercium : The Converse of Francis and his Sons with Holy Poverty. London, 1904.

Thomas of Celano. The Lives of St. Francis of Assisi. Translated by A. G. Ferrers Howell. London, 1908.

Underhill, E. Jacopone da Todi : A Spiritual Biography : with a selection from the Spiritual Songs translated by Mrs. Theodore Beck. London, 1919.

CHAPTER VI

ENGLISH MEDIÆVAL MYSTICS

RICHARD ROLLE—"THE CLOUD OF UNKNOWING"—
WALTER HILTON—JULIAN OF NORWICH

THE great English mystics form a fairly compact group. All their works were produced in the course of the fourteenth century. They begin with Richard Rolle, who died in 1349, the year of the Black Death. They end with Julian of Norwich, who seems to have completed her *Revelations* about 1393. It is a peculiarity of their writings that all are connected with the solitary or, as they called it, the " singular life," which seems at this period to have had a deep attraction for all who sought spiritual perfection. Rolle at his conversion chose the career of a hermit ; Julian of Norwich was an anchoress. *The Cloud of Unknowing* and *Scale of Perfection* were apparently addressed respectively to a male and a female recluse. All wrote in the vernacular, and were indeed among the first so to do, for Latin was still the literary tongue. They did this in order to widen their circle of appeal, for they addressed themselves, as did St. Francis and his followers, not merely to the professional clergy nor even to the educated aristocracy—who spoke and read French at least until Wyclif's day —but, as they said, to their " even-Christians " ;

that is, to the middle class, lay and religious, and especially the country population, always the home of our peculiar English earnestness.

Though Rolle is the first English writer to whom the name of mystic can reasonably be given, in the thirteenth century English religious works were already being produced, marked by impassioned Christocentric emotion. Such pieces as the well-known prose rhapsody *A Talking of the Love of God* or the immensely popular poem *Sweet Jesu, now will I sing*—an expanded imitation of the *Jesu dulcis memoria*, which includes the story of the Passion told in verse—show the trend of English personal religion in the Middle Ages. Already we notice in it that realism, homeliness, and tender feeling which shine in the mystics and constantly reappear in our devotional literature. Here, too, as with the first Franciscans, the romantic strain of contemporary secular literature, and especially ideas connected with chivalry, were reflected in the religious sphere. Such a lovely and truly mystical poem as *Quia amore langueo*—an anonymous fourteenth-century anticipation of *The Hound of Heaven*—has plainly and to its own advantage taken colour from the Anglo-Norman poetry of the time :

> In a valley of this restless mind
> I sought in mountain and in mead,
> Trusting a true love for to find.
> Upon an hill then took I heed ;
> A voice I heard, and near I yede,
> In great dolour complaining tho :
> See, dear soul, how my sides bleed :
> *Quia amore langueo.*

* * * *

I am true love that false was never ;
My sister, man's soul, I loved her thus.
Because we would in no wise dissever
I left my Kingdom glorious.
I purveyed her a palace full precious ;
She fled, I followed, I loved her so
That I suffered this pain piteous,
Quia amore langueo.

This stream of feeling, finding fullest expression
in the wide-spread cultus of the Holy Name of
Jesus, with its Franciscan ardour and intimacy,
and distinguished by an intense concentration on
the Passion, had been growing up since at least
the twelfth century. Many important works,
both in English and Latin, produced under its
influence, are probably still in manuscript. Doubtless owing much to the spread of St. Bernard's
writings, which so strongly affected the whole
course of mediæval mysticism, and further encouraged by the widely-circulated *Meditations of St.
Anselm*, and perhaps by infiltrations of Franciscan
fervour, it constituted the emotional preparation
for our great mystical epoch; helping to form the
favouring soil in which the genius of Rolle and
Hilton could grow.

In thinking of these mystics we must also
remember how much the religious and secular
atmosphere of the fourteenth century has affected
them—the atmosphere in which flourished the
Miracle plays, the Gothic sculpture, and the illuminations of the later Middle Ages. They are people
of their time, keeping close to the simplest traditional imagery, even when trying to convey to us
their most profound experiences. It is probably
to a disciple of Richard Rolle that we owe the

little book called *The Privity of the Passion*, an English version of part of the popular Franciscan work of devotion called *The Meditations of St. Bonaventura*, which greatly influenced late mediæval art. In this book a detailed picture of some episode of the Passion is placed before the mind, and described with an intensity of realism intended to play directly on the feelings, and excite contrition and love. Often, as in the scene of the Scourging of Christ, the author by his own imaginative power almost compels us to visualization :

He stood naked before them, a fair young man shameful in shape and specious in beauty, passing all earthly men. He suffered the hard, painful beating of those wicked men in his tenderest flesh and cleanest. Flower of all flesh and of all mankind is now full of blow-beatings. . . . When they leased him from the pillar, he yode about seeking his clothes that were casten here and there when he was first naked. Behold him here busily, thus beaten and all trembling for cold : for, as the gospel says, the time was cold.

The fact that this bit of vivid prose comes to us from the English mystical school gives some idea of the food which nourished Rolle and his followers ; the religious conceptions which filled their minds. So, too, many close correspondences with contemporary art can be found in Julian of Norwich, whose visions of the Passion have the same pictorial quality and often remind us of the paintings of the East Anglian school.

To these devotional and artistic influences, received by the English mystics from the Church within which they lived, and providing them with their spiritual landscape and atmosphere, we must add a third ; that of the Christian culture of Western Europe. This reached them through the books they read, and deeply affected the way in which they tried to impart their experience of God. They were educated persons, acquainted with a wide range of literature, uniting them with the great body of Christian feeling and thought. Indeed, their work is so full of quotations from St. Augustine, St. Gregory, St. Bernard, Hugh and Richard of St. Victor, St. Bonaventura, and other favourite authorities, that only the most exact scholarship can separate their borrowings from their creations. Thus when the author of *The Cloud of Unknowing* suddenly says " Short prayer pierceth heaven ! " we might suppose this to be one of the original epigrams which abound in his writing ; but he is merely translating St. Augustine word for word. So too with their other sources ; they take phrases and ideas from the great masters who have preceded them, and weave these dexterously into their own work. Above all, Rolle and Hilton are saturated in the language and imagery of the Bible, and a close knowledge of Scripture is needed if we are to understand all their words imply. They constantly insert texts from the Vulgate, and these texts they generally translate. In fact, Bible reading, sometimes considered peculiarly charac-teristic of English piety, is historically the child of mysticism. Richard Rolle was the first to translate the Psalter into English ; and exhorts his disciples that they " be not negligent in meditating and reading holy Scripture, and most in those places where it teaches manners and to eschew deceits of the fiend and speaks of God's love and contemplative living " ; and we can get from the English mystics a considerable collection of vernacular Scripture passages, which they had put in circulation before Wyclif's day. Thus the great English mystics were firmly rooted in the religious, social and artistic life of their time ; their lives and works were not merely individual expressions of fervour, but arose within, and contributed to the general Christian consciousness of the Church. Differing widely in temperament and so in outlook, this contribution had in each a special novelty and freshness of its own.

We may truly say of the first, Richard Rolle of Hampole, that he started a new stream of spiritual life in England ; and that all the others depend to some extent on him. A Yorkshire boy, probably born in the reign of Edward I, he seems to have been well connected, had powerful friends, and became an Oxford scholar. His works—for he wrote much, both in Latin and English—show that he loved letters, that he was a natural poet, and that music was one of the passions of his life. He was on fire with spiritual ecstasy, and translated it best into musical form. " My heart Thou hast bound in love of Thy Name, and now I cannot but sing it ! "

Perhaps it was at Oxford that he came under the Franciscan influence which is recognizable in his life and work. He had many of the characteristics of St. Francis : the unconventional outlook, the alternating moods of penitence and joy, the mingled homeliness and transcendentalism, the love of song and of natural things, the intense devotion to the Holy Name. The sudden and thorough way in which he abandoned his whole worldly career and embraced poverty, his hauntings of country places, the combination in him of missionary and poet, the personal quality of his mysticism —all these seem like the transplanting into the bracing Yorkshire air of those dispositions which were shown in perfection at Assisi. Like Francis, Rolle never took orders ; he is, indeed, one of the most unclerical and independent of the Catholic mystics. True, he lacked the childlike and gentle outlook of his pattern, was combative as well as romantic, and perhaps deficient in personal charm. But the crucial act of his life had so Franciscan a character, that we are almost tempted to read into it the influence, direct or indirect, of the swiftly-spreading legend of the Saint.

He was eighteen when, abruptly returning from Oxford to his Yorkshire home, he abandoned the career of scholarship, made himself a hermit's gown of grey and white from two of his sister's old tunics, and, as he afterwards said, " fled that which me confused," obeying the overwhelming desire of the religious genius for a lonely and simple life in which his spiritual instincts could find room to grow. Years afterwards he described his state of mind in words which almost seem to give us the very accents of Francis :

In the beginning truly of my conversion and singular purpose I thought I would be like the little bird that for love of its lover longs ; but in her longing she is gladdened when he comes that she loves. And joying she sings, and singing she longs, but in sweetness and heat. It is said the nightingale to song and melody all night is given, that she may please him to whom she is joined. How mickle more with greatest sweetness to Christ my Jesu should I sing, that is spouse of my soul, by all this present life that is night in regard of clearness to come.

From this time Rolle seems to have lived the life of a hermit-missionary, sometimes wandering from place to place preaching and giving counsel, sometimes sitting long hours in his cell immersed in communion with the love that filled his mind, as he said, with " heavenly melody." It seems certain that the early stages of his spiritual life were marked by abnormal psychological experiences. He tells us that nearly three years after his " life-changing "—years doubtless spent in self-discipline and moral struggle—the " heavenly door " was opened to him, " so that the eyes of the heart might behold and see what way they might seek my Love."

The door stayed open ; and about a year later he experienced the first of the three states of spiritual joy which he calls Heat, Sweetness, and Song. As he sat meditating in a chapel he suddenly felt in his heart " a merry heat and unknown " ; so intense, that at first he " groped his breast," thinking it had a material origin. Such a translation of emotional fervour into physical terms, though not common, is mentioned by many ascetic writers and explained by psychology. Rolle had continued for fifteen months in this " feeling of burning love," when he developed his characteristic form of mystical experience. Sitting one evening in the same chapel, saying his psalms, and " praying to heaven with his whole desire," suddenly he felt within himself the welling up of a mysterious heavenly music, which dwelt continually in his mind, so that his prayers and meditations were turned into song. Henceforward his communion with the spiritual world was most

often expressed in musical terms, as an outpouring
melody of joy and praise. From this burning love
and " inshed melody "—for he realized that it
could not be produced by his own powers—proceeded the " sweetness untrowed " which completed
the transfiguration of his soul.

In these three, that are tokens of love most perfect, the high
perfection of Christian religion without all doubt is found . . .
nevertheless to the saints that have shone in them I dare not make
myself even, for they peradventure more perfectly them have
received. Yet shall I be busy with virtue that I may more burningly
love, more sweetly sing, the sweetness of love more plenteously feel.

There seems no reason why we should refuse
to accept this account of the " happy heat, sweetness desired, and joyful song " which expressed
Rolle's adoring apprehensions of God. He was
a genuine religious genius, intensely susceptible to
spiritual impressions, and easily giving them sensible
form. His mystical life was full and well balanced,
moving between the poles of stern discipline and
thrilling joy. We might call him the Shelley of
English mysticism : most fully expressing the
delight of a poet who has found the untarnished
source of beauty and love. Rolle's exclamation,
" Nought merrier than grace of contemplation ! "
may strike oddly on the modern ear, but we
cannot doubt that it represents his own attitude.
Yet this ardour and poetry conceal a strong, sane
and well-nourished spirituality ; a robust and
practical moral sense. Rolle developed and taught
the three-fold response to God which is characteristic of the full religious nature, finding Him
immanent in other men—since, " if our love be
pure and perfect, whatever our heart loves, it is

God " ; fully realized and adored in terms of self-giving personality in the worship of the Holy Name ; and finally discerned dimly in His transcendent mystery in the " divine ignorance " of contemplation. " As we standing in darkness see nothing, so in contemplation that invisibly lightens the soul, no light is seen."

Again, he was an exacting moralist, keenly aware that the healthy inner life is based upon ethics, and unpurified ardours must always be suspect. To read his moral treatises or those of his disciples is to re-enter the world of the late Middle Ages in the company of an acute and often amusing guide, and find much we can recognize in the way of weakness or excess. Whilst never disguising his own preference for a purely contemplative life " set towards the light unseen with great desire," yet his love compelled him to action. He taught, wrote, gathered disciples ; and required that he who was really " kindled by God's fire " should not only " pay Christ praise in ghostly music, but also stir others to love." This indeed he did and still can do. His mysticism was not only personal, but creative ; the whole English school really descends from it, and, at least in the north, it brought into being a genuine revival of the spiritual life.

Rolle represents for his day almost the extreme of individualism possible to a mystic who remained obedient to the Church. He passionately proclaimed liberty of conscience, declaring himself to be directed by the Holy Ghost ; and the Lollards of the next generation claimed for their doctrines the support of his words. Though his teaching is solidly based on St. Augustine, St. Anselm, St. Bernard, Richard of St. Victor, still all is coloured by his ardent temperament. He was, and remained, something of a free lance.

The next great English mystic, probably writing towards the end of Rolle's life, was of a different type. If Rolle represents the emotional and poetic extreme of mysticism, he represents its philosophic pole. He was certainly a theologian, perhaps a cloistered monk, and his chief work, *The Cloud of Unknowing*, was addressed to a young recluse who had chosen, like Rolle, "singular living." He also wrote four little tracts on special aspects of the inner life, and was probably the author of *Dionise Hid Divinite*, an English translation of the *Mystical Theology* of Dionysius the Areopagite, which had an immense influence on the development of our native mysticism.

The author of *The Cloud* was clearly a great contemplative, loving silence and tranquillity ; yet also an experienced director of souls, full of the sturdy English practicality, here carried into the most secret places of the spirit, and a keen and humorous—even irritable—observer of his fellow-men. If Rolle and Hilton show us the English layman of the fourteenth century as his spiritual teachers saw him, we get from this nameless mystic a vigorous and amusing picture of the fourteenth-century cloister, with its ardent, sanctimonious, hypocritical, fidgety, and variously tiresome inhabitants. We see through his eyes the "young presumptuous disciples" whose conceited mysticality "will with curiosity of imagination pierce the planets, and make an hole in the firmament to look in thereat " ; the religious emotionalists who " travail their fleshly hearts outrageously in their breasts, and hurt full sore the silly soul and make it fester in fantasy feigned of fiends." Both types are offensive to that sober sense of reality by which he proves himself a true mystic. He likes a quiet style in spiritual persons, but seldom gets it. Basing his remarks upon a passage in Hugh of St. Victor, he describes the mannerisms of his fellow-religious in a spirit hardly consistent with that " charity of meekness " which he recommends :

Some persons are so cumbered in nice curious customs in bodily bearing that when they shall aught to hear, they writhe their heads on one side quaintly, and up with the chin ; they gape with their mouths as they should hear with their mouths and not with their ears. Some when they should speak point with their fingers, either on their fingers or on their own breasts or on theirs that they speak to. Some can neither sit still, stand still nor lie still, unless they be either wagging with their feet or else somewhat doing with their hands. Some row with their arms in time of their speaking, as them needed for to swim over a great water. Some be ever more smiling and laughing at every other word that they speak, as they were giggling girls and nice japing jugglers lacking behaviour.

These tricks, he allows, are not great sins ; but he mentions them because they are " tokens of unstableness of heart and unrestfulness of mind." He particularly dislikes the clerical manner, " with many meek piping words and gestures of devotion." Real spirituality, he thinks, makes people so pleasant " that each good man that them saw should be fain and joyful to have them in company," and this natural courtesy and seemliness ought also to mark their religious behaviour. " Learn to love listily, with a soft and demure behaviour as well in body as in soul, and snatch not over hastily, as it were a greedy greyhound, hunger thee never so sore."

So much for the human interest of this writer. His mystical teaching is based on " Dionysius the Areopagite," whose profound conception of God as transcending all thought and all categories he translates into practical terms. The Divine Presence is hid in a " cloud of unknowing," which can only be pierced by " a sharp dart of longing love . . . speedily springing unto God as a sparkle from the' coal." That strange outstretching of the soul in prayer to Something which is beyond itself—which can, as it were, be apprehended as a whole " by the true lovely will of the heart " but never be conceived by the mind—is wonderfully suggested by him :

> For of all other creatures and their works, yea, and of the works of God's self, may a man through grace have full-head of knowing, and well he can think of them : but of God Himself can no man think. And therefore I would leave all that thing that I can think, and choose to my love that thing that I cannot think. For why ; He may well be loved, but not thought. By love may He be gotten and holden ; but by thought never. And therefore, although it be good sometime to think of the kindness and the worthiness of God in special, and although it be a light and a part of contemplation : nevertheless yet in this work it shall be cast down and covered with a cloud of forgetting. And thou shalt step above it stalwartly, but listily, with a devout and a pleasing stirring of love, and try for to pierce that darkness above thee. And smite upon that thick cloud of unknowing with a sharp dart of longing love ; and go not thence for thing that befalleth.

But this austere Neoplatonic conception of the unknowable Godhead is transformed by the English genius for homeliness ; which is nowhere more strikingly apparent than in this transcendental book, with its distrust of " curiosity of clergy and letterly cunning as in clerks," and its constant recourse to simplest human imagery. Take, for instance, the beautiful little passage which pictures the Divine mercy descending on a despairing soul " for to take thee up, and cherishly dry thine ghostly eyen, as the father doth the child that is in point to perish under the mouths of wild swine, or wode biting bears."

The writer's constant dissociation of spirituality from the categories of space and time, reminding us that " nowhere bodily is everywhere ghostly," that " heaven ghostly is as nigh down as up and up as down," and " the high and the best way thither is run by desires and not by paces of feet," his refusal to attribute value to " any long psalter unmindfully mumbled in the teeth," his sturdy, constant demands for " listy " behaviour—namely eager, willing activity, the opposite of listless— with the crisply practical advice to " do forth ever more and more, so that thou be ever doing " and " look now forwards, and let be backwards " since " a good will is the substance of all perfection "—all these characters give him a marked individuality among the mystics.

The language and attitude of Richard Rolle were coloured by poetry ; those of the writer of *The Cloud* by mystical philosophy. The third of the great English mystics, Walter Hilton, occupies a central position between them. An educated theologian, he is familiar with the work of both his predecessors, and with their literary sources too, especially SS. Augustine, Gregory and Bernard ; but his attitude is more pastoral, his language even more warmly Christocentric than theirs, his writing more saturated with Biblical imagery. Hilton was in the strict sense neither monk nor recluse. He was an Augustinian canon, an inmate of the important priory of Thurgarton, and familiar with the normal social life of his day. His career covered the second half of the fourteenth century, and he died in 1396. He was thus contemporary with Julian of Norwich, who was born about 1342 and still living in 1413, and her work shows traces of his influence. He lived through the period of Wyclif, and echoes of the Lollard controversy can be detected in his chief book.

The Cloud of Unknowing was addressed to those who had chosen a contemplative life and had a natural disposition for it : to others, its author says, " this matter accordeth nothing." And as to ordinary imperfect humanity he was even more emphatic : " Fleshly janglers, open praisers and blamers of themselves or of any other, tellers of trifles, gossips and tattlers of tales, and all manner of pinchers, cared I never that they saw this book." But Walter Hilton, though his principal work, *The Scale of Perfection*, was addressed to an anchoress, shows a more tolerant and genial spirit. He is a real shepherd of souls ; and in his *Treatise on Mixed Life* has given us the perfect guide to the mysticism of ordinary men. Less of a poet than Rolle, he is far more of a psychologist—a deep, wide, tender, yet delicately discriminative mind. *The Scale of Perfection* is a complete way-book of the spiritual life, from its simplest beginnings to its ineffable end. Hilton thinks of it, characteristically, under two complementary metaphors : as a complete re-making of human personality, or " re-forming " of the lost divine image in the soul, and as a journey, a pilgrimage to Jerusalem "which betokeneth the perfect love of God set on the hill of contemplation." Under the one he is able to emphasize the need for a drastic purification of character, under the other the courage and un-divided concentration of purpose demanded of those who undertake the adventures of the mystic way. He knows, and never forgets, the facts of human nature, and often startles us by his shrewd analysis of our common weaknesses and self-deceptions, his uncanny psychological insight. He looks past conduct to its source, and insists on a drastic purification of motive; refusing to be satisfied by outward renunciations and good deeds if " the great spring of love unto thyself " still rises secretly in the soul. In this case " Thou art like unto a man which had in his garden a stinking well with many runnels from it. He went and stopped the runnels and left the spring whole, and weened all had been secure. But the water sprung up at the ground of the well and stood still, so mickle that it corrupted all the fairness of the garden." It is not surprising that *The Scale of Perfection* remained for centuries the most popular of English spiritual works, for most of its counsels are still as appropriate to our needs as to those of the fourteenth century. With his master, St. Augustine, Hilton bases the spiritual life on the twin virtues of meekness and love ; conceiving of man's entrance into union with God as a gradual education in these. Meekness, he thinks, is simply spiritual realism, or self-knowledge ; love, " that is both the Giver and the gift," the one quality that is both human and divine. " Therefore shape thee for to be arrayed in His likeness, that is in meekness and charity, which is His livery ; and then will He homely know thee, and show to thee His privity."

Such a mysticism is not merely philosophic, cloistered, nor ecstatic ; it invites the ordinary man or woman, and bears upon the simplest duties of existence. Hilton condemns the spirituality which neglects practical tasks—care of children, servants, tenants or the poor—in order to luxuriate in contemplation ; calling it bluntly, as St. Augustine had done, " tending God's head and neglecting His feet." " Surely He will more thank thee for the humble washing of His feet, when they are very foul and yield an ill savour to thee, than for all the curious painting and fair dressing or decking that thou canst make about His head by devoutest remembrance ? " Nevertheless this robust spirituality has behind it a heavenly vision, and I think we must add a heavenly experience, not dissimilar from that which inspired Richard Rolle. Most of Hilton's mystical pieces are still in manuscript ; but one, the lovely *Song of Angels*, was published by Wynken de Worde and has since been reprinted. It shows that the sense of the musical quality of spiritual joy which was Rolle's most famous characteristic was also felt by his successor. Its language proves how entirely Hilton must be reckoned a disciple of Rolle, whose favourite phrases he often repeats, and whose insistence on the need of discriminating between the self-deceptions of the sham mystic, and the real perception of spiritual things, he emphasizes in this piece. " Sometimes," says Hilton, " a man gathereth his own wits by violence to seek and to behold heavenly things . . . and over travaileth by imagination his wits and by indiscreet travailling turneth the brains in his head. . . . And then for feebleness of brain he thinketh that he heareth wonderful sounds and songs, and that is nothing else than a fantasy, caused of troubling of the brain." And, as the final expression of that sanctified common sense which is always a mark of the real mystic, he concludes on these golden words : " It sufficeth to me for to live in truth principally, and not in feeling."

The last of our four great English mystics, Julian of Norwich, stands out with peculiar distinctness. As the first real English woman of letters, she has special interest for us : the more so when we consider the beauty of character, depth of thought, and poetic feeling which her one book displays. In her mingled homeliness and philosophic instinct, her passion for Nature, her profound devotion to the Holy Name, she represents all the best elements of English mysticism. We feel in her the literary culmination of the Gothic spirit : the sense of mystery, delicate beauty, and robust contact with the common life, which meet us in the cathedrals ; the vivid human sympathy with the mysteries of the Passion, yet the natural gaiety and homeliness, which inspired those miniature painters of the thirteenth and fourteenth centuries who form part of the cultural surroundings in which her genius flowered.

Apparently the most subjective, Julian is really the most philosophic of our early mystics : an attractive and also an astonishing figure. Internal evidence proves that she was a Norfolk gentle-woman of considerable education, though she humbly describes herself as simple and unlettered. She was born about 1343, in the reign of Edward III. In spite of the wonderful atmosphere of joy which transfigures her writing, her invul-nerable conviction that the universe, when we come to understand it, will be found to be good and rational through and through, her early life was not happy. She says she often desired death because "for sloth and weakness I liked not to live and travail, as fell me to do." As a girl she prayed that she might have an illness at thirty years of age, and closer understanding of the Passion. The illness came at the right time : a fact which indicates Julian's psychic suggestibility. At its crisis she fell into a trance lasting five hours, and in this received the visions of the Passion and the spiritual revelations which form the foundation of her book. All that she after-wards wrote was the result of meditation on this experience; in which she found ever more meaning with the passing years, and her own growth in insight and knowledge.

It is a mistake to regard Julian's book as the mere outpouring of an ecstatic, the uncriticized record of the working of her subconscious mind. Like her predecessors, St. Hildegarde and Angela of Foligno, she was intelligent and well-informed, and pondered much upon her mystical experience. Her *Revelations of Divine Love* exist in two forms :

a short version, perhaps written soon after the visions were received, a long version, composed twenty years after this experience. Analysis shows how greatly Julian's outlook had developed in the interval ; how numerous the literary sources drawn upon in order to explicate the meanings she had discovered in the "ghostly words" heard long before in her mind. The difference between the first experience and the finished product is much like the difference we must presume between St. Augustine's highly finished *Confessions* and the actual events they record. As an anchoress, she was obliged by her rule to spend part of each day in such reading as her education allowed ; and it is clear that from such reading, sermons, or conversation she had learned a considerable amount of that Christian Platonism which came through St. Augustine into the mediæval Church. She obviously knew Hilton's work, and sometimes reminds us of her great contemporaries, Suso, Tauler and Ruysbroeck.

In her combination of soaring philosophy with homely simplicity Julian resembles and excels the great Franciscan mystics. She is truly Christian in her power of including transcendence and humanity in her sweep, and this she is able to do because of her peculiar and vivid consciousness of the changeless, all-penetrative, yet simple action of God.

In this same time our Lord showed me a ghostly sight of His homely loving. I saw that He is to us everything that is good and comfortable for us ; He is our clothing that for love wrappeth us, claspeth us and all becloseth us for tender love, that He may never leave us ; being to us all-thing that is good, as to mine understanding.

THE MYSTICS OF THE CHURCH

. . . And after this I saw God in a point, that is to say in mine understanding, by which sight I saw that He is in all things. . . . Wherefore me behoveth needs to grant that all-thing that is done, it is well done : for our Lord God doeth all. For in this time the working of creatures was not shewed, but of our Lord God in the creature : for He is the mid-point of all thing and all He doth. . . . God is nature in His being, that is to say, the goodness that is in nature, this is God. He is the ground, He is the substance, He is the same thing that is Naturehood.

In such passages we are with the philosophers. But it is a vivid picture of home life, not the lofty speculations of Christian metaphysic, which Julian gives us when she says :

A child, when it is a-hurt or adread, it runneth hastily to the mother for help, with all its might. So willeth He that we do, as a meek child saying thus, " My kind mother, my gracious mother, my dearworthy mother, have mercy on me ! I have made myself foul and unlike thee, and I nor may nor can amend it but with thy help !

This sweet and homely sense that most men are spiritual babies, and that human sins and mistakes are best dealt with from this point of view, is found in Julian again and again. It is part of her tender-hearted and generous sense of humanity. Men, she thinks, are all thoroughly lovable, in spite of their weaknesses and sins. A " saint " is not, to her seeing, an anæmic, thin creature, the amateur of an impossible perfection; but a real human being who has often done real bad things, yet whose sins and imperfections have been transcended, and become in her paradoxical phrase " not wounds but honours." " Mine understanding," she says, " was lifted up into heaven, and then God brought merrily to my mind David and others in the old law without number "—personages, we must agree, not distinguished by a prudish moral sense. It was a great joy to Julian to feel that heaven was as wide and tolerant as her own great heart. Yet she never minimizes evil or descends to a merely sentimental optimism. " Our failing," she says, " is dreadful, our falling is shameful, and our dying is sorrowful. But in all this the sweet eye of pity and love cometh never off us, nor the working of mercy ceaseth not." In this last quotation we have an example of the perfect fusion of feeling and expression which Julian displays in her best passages. She is a great stylist, in spite of the fact that we see in her that passion for significant numbers which is so often allied with the mystical temperament. Her arguments and images always fall into threes. " For all our life," she says, " is in three. In the first we have our being, in the second we have our increasing, and in the third we have our fulfilling. The first is Nature, the second is Mercy, and the third is Grace." And in her culminating vision of reality she declares its properties to be three : Life, Love and Light.

> In life is marvellous homeliness, and in love is gentle courtesy and in light is endless Nature-hood. These properties were in the Goodness : unto which Goodness my reason would be oned, and cleave to it with all my might.

Julian's work forms a fitting crown to the golden period of English mysticism. Though she seems, and indeed is, so strongly individual, yet she is also in the best sense fully traditional. Even her loftiest flights do not represent an escape from the common religious environment, but rather the artist's power of feeding on it and discovering in it more and more beauty, reality and depth.

" From the beginning to the end," she says in a passage which well describes the classic relation of the mystic to the Church, " I had two manners of beholding. The one was endless, continuant love, with secureness of keeping and blissful salvation, for of this was all the shewing. The other was of the common teaching of Holy Church in which I was afore informed and grounded, and with all my will having in use and understanding. And the beholding of this went not from me : for by the shewing I was not stirred nor led therefrom in no manner of point, but I had therein teaching to love it and like it : whereby I might, by the help of our Lord and His grace, increase and rise to more heavenly knowing and higher loving."

ILLUSTRATIVE WORKS

Cloud of Unknowing, The. Edited by E. Underhill. London, 1912.

Gardner, Edmund. The Cell of Self-Knowledge : Seven Old English Mystical Works. London, 1910.

Hilton, Walter. The Scale of Perfection. Edited by E. Underhill. London, 1923.

Horstman, C. Richard Rolle of Hampole and his Followers. 2 vols. London, 1895.

Julian of Norwich. Revelations of Divine Love. Edited by Grace Warrack. London, 1901.

Comfortable Words for Christ's Lovers. Edited by the Rev. Dundas Harford. London, 1911.

Rolle, Richard. The Fire of Love and the Mending of Life. Edited by F. Comper. London, 1914.

The Form of Perfect Living. Edited by Dr. Geraldine Hodgson. London, 1910.

CHAPTER VII

GERMAN AND FLEMISH MYSTICISM

ECKHART—THE FRIENDS OF GOD—"THEOLOGIA
GERMANICA"—TÁULER—SUSO—RUYSBROECK

THE expansion of mystical religion in mediæval
Italy and England was largely due to the spiritual
experience of St. Francis and of Richard Rolle :
an experience coloured by romanticism, by a sharp
revolt from religious conventions, by an ardent
and personal Christocentric feeling. In both we
see the characteristic reaction of a poetic and
artistic temperament to Eternal Life. The man
who has been justly called the Father of German
Mysticism was of a very different type, but the
life-giving character of his great personality was
not less marked. All that is peculiar in the teaching of the German mystics, differentiating it from
the general Christian tradition of the inner life,
originates in the teaching of Meister Eckhart.
His daring—indeed sometimes dangerous—speculations and profound insights brought to the
spiritual landscape of the later Middle Ages new
mystery and depth ; and, in spite of exaggerations,
greatly enriched and spiritualized the general " sense
of God."

Born about 1260, Eckhart entered the Dominican order as a youth, and studied at Cologne and
at Paris; theological schools in which the influence

of the great Dominican doctors, Albertus Magnus (1193–1280) and his pupil St. Thomas Aquinas (1225–74), was paramount. Eckhart learnt much from these sources, and frequently quotes St. Thomas's works ; but the determining fact in his mental formation was his encounter with Neo-platonic philosophy, so exactly appropriate to his intensely religious yet fastidious and speculative mind. He owed much to Dionysius the Areo-pagite, and perhaps to the great though heretical genius of Erigena. Pure and unworldly, with a remarkable instinct for metaphysical realities, and an intellectual passion for clearness even in the most ineffable reaches of spiritual experience, he pushed to an extreme that Neoplatonic conception of Reality which has always formed a part, but never the whole, of the mystical tradition of the Church. It encouraged in him a total disdain for history and succession, a tendency to exile God from His creation ; and led him to set up a sharp distinction between the Absolute and unconditioned Godhead, " unknown and never to be known," and the God of religious experience. This separa-tion is fundamental to Eckhart's thought, and affected the whole development of German mysti-cism.

Yet this leaning to transcendental speculation, landing him at last in a monism which—did we judge him by his formal declarations—can hardly be reconciled with Christianity, was combined with simple and homely pastoral effort. Intellec-tual processes might lead to the discovery of a " bare " and impersonal Divinity, unoccupied with time and space, and to the logical demand for a

similar abstraction on the part of " sanctified "
souls. But a deep religious sensitiveness modified
this inhuman aloofness. The vernacular sermons,
preached mostly to the laity and religious communities of Strassburg, by which we know Eckhart
best, are a strange blend of metaphysical and
missionary fervour, exhibiting by turns the influence of his heart and his head. With his gaze, as
it were, perpetually fixed beyond the horizons of
the mind, he set forth the most abstract of conceptions with the persuasive ardour of a lover.
Even now we cannot read him without catching
something of his certitude that only the Unknowable is truly real and truly to be desired.

He preached to those who could bear it—and
his immense reputation testifies to the general
hunger for a deepening of spiritual life—the
austere doctrine of total detachment from creatures.
He insisted that " if a soul is to see God it must
look at nothing in time ; for while the soul is
occupied with time or place or any image of the
kind, it cannot recognize God. . . . Only he
knows God who recognizes that all creatures are
nothingness." By this constant emphasis on the
mystery of Being, the unsearchableness of the real
things of God, Eckhart revived that sense of awe
which is fundamental to the spiritual life. Yet
against this unplumbed background of the Infinite
he displays a divine love which is " ever ready,
though we are unready—nigh to us, though we
are far from Him," and is discoverable as surely
by the path of mercy as by that of contemplation.
" Were one in a rapture like that of St. Paul," he
says, " and a sick man needed help, it were better

to come out of the rapture and show love by serving him who had need."

Though the judgment of the Pope upon Eckhart, that " he wished to know more than he should," is not born of mere obscurantism, but contains sound common sense, there is no doubt that his violent and one-sided restatement of the foundations of theism—his struggle to make diagrams of the undiscoverable—did real service to the inner life of the Church. He ranks with the creative mystics whose experience of God has quickened other souls, and through them enriched the general Christian consciousness.

The distinctive fact about the German mystics of the fourteenth century is the enormous impulse they received from Eckhart, their close acquaintance with his teaching ; all use his ideas, modified and warmed through by their own temperament or experience. From him they get their wide horizons, their way of escape from a merely human range of imagery and emotion. This is specially true of his two chief disciples, the Dominicans Suso (c. 1295–1365) and Tauler (c. 1300–61), whose immense veneration for their " Great Master " indicates the strength of Eckhart's personality and the devotion he could inspire. In Suso, Eckhartian theology is combined with the ascetic and monastic tradition, and passed through a singularly gentle, fervent, and romantic mind. In Tauler we see a born preacher and reformer turning the same material to his special purposes. The Fleming, Ruysbroeck (1293–1381), one of the greatest of Christian contemplatives, seems often to use Eckhart's ideas as a means of expressing his own experiences, but the ardour and realism with which he invests them are his own.

With this group of mystics, all young men at the time of Eckhart's death, and all strongly affected by him, we encounter the second, or social phase of German mysticism. Suso and Tauler were directly, Ruysbroeck perhaps indirectly, connected wtih the widespread spiritual movement, or revival, of the Friends of God, which incorporated everything that was best in the personal and active religion of the time. As the Spiritual Franciscans strove to perpetuate the inner teaching and apostolic ardour of St. Francis, and actually provided a religious environment in which mysticism could grow; so this informal brotherhood, largely of lay origin and membership, fed upon the stern Eckhartian teaching and became a nursery of visionaries and mystics.

Like the Spiritual Franciscans, the Friends of God were and desired to remain faithful members of the Catholic Church ; but they put before tradition the direct experiences of the Spirit. They had, too, an apocalyptic side to their propaganda, revealing their attachment to that German prophetic tradition which began with St. Hildegarde. They denounced the numerous and glaring abuses and sins of the time, foretold divine vengeance, demanded realism and sincerity, and practised an often extreme asceticism; regarding themselves as an " inner Church " of spiritual men, a faithful remnant in an evil generation, directly guided by the Holy Ghost. They taught a mystical form of personal religion, based on the conception of a " divine spark " or Godlike quality latent in every soul, by the upgrowth of which those called to experience God might become " divine and super-natural men." These were said to be led into " the Upper School of Perfect Resignation," where great trials and sufferings were endured, selfhood was slain, and the Holy Spirit was felt to be teaching directly within the soul. In this doctrine of the Inner Light, the Friends of God anticipated the Quaker position ; but they never broke with institutional religion, and seem to have felt peculiar reverence for the sacraments.

Such a spiritual atmosphere inevitably produced a large crop of abnormal phenomena. Ecstasy, visions, prophecy and clairvoyance became frequent among the members of the group. A quantity of literature—much of it still in existence—was produced and circulated among the members, who were scattered through the Rhineland, Switzer-land and Bavaria. This literature, which is partly allegorical and prophetic, partly confessional and didactic, and abounds in psychological and his-torical problems, indicates that, whilst Dominican influence was prominent, the direction and inspira-tion of the Friends of God remained largely in lay hands. In a time of much clerical corruption, the movement asserted the right of the truly spiritual man to assume religious leadership and teach religious truth. Thus one of its leaders was Rulman Merswin, a Strassburg merchant, whose spiritual experiences are recorded in the *Book of Nine Rocks*. The ideal figure of the " Friend of God of the Oberland," prominent in its documents, is a layman ; whilst the *Book of the Master of Holy Scripture* is designed to show that even a great theologian may learn supernatural truth from any holy but unlearned man.

We may therefore regard the movement of the Friends of God as an unorganized corporate experiment in mystical religion, fed on the intellectual side by Eckhart, on the prophetic and visionary side by the older German mysticism. The ecstatic nuns, Margaret and Christina Ebner, who were amongst its leaders, reproduced many of the characteristics of St. Hildegarde. We see in the wonderful little book called the *Theologia Germanica* the strength and beauty of the spiritual teaching which nourished it. Here the Neoplatonic demand for a total flight from created things, in order that the uncreated and eternal may be achieved, is reinterpreted in terms of will and desire. It is through the fixing of these powers of the soul upon Reality—that is to say a total and selfless concentration on the purposes of God—that man escapes from the fetters of mere selfhood; and, " made a partaker of the Divine Nature," finds his true personality and peace.

He who is made a partaker of the Divine Nature neither willeth, desireth nor seeketh anything save Goodness as Goodness for the sake of Goodness . . . where this Light is, the man's end and aim is not this or that, Me or Thee, or the like, but only the One, Who is neither I nor Thou, this nor that, but is above all I and Thou, this and that; and in Him all goodness is loved as one Good.

This solid and bracing doctrine, with its sure touch upon the supernatural, its easy movement between the homely and the transcendent, shows us the mysticism of the Friends of God at its best : its spiritual realism, its moral zeal. The anonymous writer, through whom these ideas passed to

Luther and thence into the main stream of Protestant thought, is described as a priest of the Teutonic order in Frankfort. He was plainly influenced by Eckhart, and more directly by his pupil Tauler, the greatest personality among the leaders of the Friends of God.

Through Tauler, the movement maintained that contact with the great spiritual traditions of Christendom which saved it from degenerating into the fanatical extravagances of many contemporary mystical sects. Though we know little of him beyond what his vernacular sermons tell us—for the other works ascribed to him are not considered authentic—these sermons, of which nearly a hundred and fifty survive, entitle him to a great place among the teaching mystics of the Church. Born about 1300, he became a Dominican novice at fifteen, and during his studies at Strassburg and Cologne came under the influence of Eckhart, whose teaching permanently coloured his thought. He lived for a time in Basle, a great centre of the Friends of God; afterwards returning to Strassburg, where he died in 1361.

Tauler unites a deep philosophic mysticism with intense pastoral fervour. His sermons, with their evidences of religious culture, their close dependence on St. Augustine, St. Bernard and St. Thomas Aquinas, their easy movement between the simplest religious imagery and the loftiest mystical ideas, witness to the greatness and steadiness of his soul. He invests the profound conception of the Godhead which he learned from Eckhart with a warmth of appeal which brings it within the radius of simple Christian experience : for " the depth of the

Divine Abyss cannot be fathomed by reason, but the depth may be fathomed by deep humility." All good and humble men, he thinks, should be able, "communing with themselves in their inmost hearts," thus to "return to the Source from which we sprang." Such a "return to thine Origin means that the presence of all things in which thou canst not find God will seem like a wound to thee," and it requires a complete detachment from personal desire.

Tauler's demands on those who chose the spiritual life were heroic in their completeness. He asked of them "a mind that is empty and untroubled by *all* other things, and has secretly yielded itself up with *all* its powers in the Presence of God." To one who really achieved this, he declared that "many a glimpse will be vouchsafed in his inmost heart ; and what God is will be made much clearer and plainer to him than the natural sun is to his bodily eyes."

In such passages Tauler seems to give us a hint of his own mystical experiences, as to which his reticence is otherwise complete : for his method is always objective. Though he can speak more wonderfully perhaps than any mystic since St. Augustine of that unconditioned experience of God beyond thought, which is "so close and yet so far off, and so far beyond all things that it has neither time nor place—a simple and unchanging condition," yet his language remains impersonal, and offers no encouragement to that cult of religious consolations which often flourishes in coteries of the devout. To his mind the true Friend of God was one who had chosen for friendship's sake a hard career, and might even rise beyond acceptance to a " consuming thirst " for suffering. " That a man should have a life of quiet or rest in God is good ; that a man should lead a painful life in patience is better ; but that a man should have rest in a painful life is best of all ! " Here the doctrine of unmitigated detachment justifies itself, and is brought back into immediate touch with the tensions and opportunities of human life.

If Tauler taught, and teaches still, by exclusively objective methods, his friend and contemporary Suso redresses the balance by the vividly personal and subjective character of his work. In his autobiography he reveals, almost without reserve, the course of his interior life; showing in action the principles which Tauler expounds. He too was a Dominican friar, and had sat at the feet of Eckhart, whose influence is easily recognized in the philosophic passages of his *Life*, and especially in the *Book of Eternal Wisdom*. After Eckhart's death Suso had a vision in which that " Blessed Master "—whose most daring propositions were destined to be censured by the Church—appeared, and signified that he was in great glory, and that his soul was " transformed and made Godlike in God."

Upon this the Servitor besought him to tell him two things. The first was, the manner in which those persons dwell in God, who with real and genuine detachment have sought to rest in the supreme Truth alone ? To this he answered, that no words can tell the way in which these persons are taken up into the modeless abyss of the Divine Essence. The second thing was : what exercise is most calculated to help forward him, whose earnest desire is to arrive at this state ? The Master replied that he must die to himself by deep detachment, receive everything as from God and not from creatures, and establish himself in unruffled patience towards all men, however wolfish they may be.

But in spite of his veneration for Eckhart, Suso's real affinities were with the earlier German mystics. The poetic and symbolic visions of St. Mechthild and St. Gertrude, their turn for dramatic action, their ardent yet innocent emotionalism, are more congenial to him than the austere doctrine of the unknowable Godhead. He tells us very simply that " he had from youth up a loving heart " ; and from the time of his conversion—which happened when he was eighteen—this governed his religious reactions. Like his contemporary, Richard Rolle, he loved to describe in almost sensual terms the sweet savour, ardent fires and heavenly music which visited his adoring soul. Songs and dances, flowers and angels, all the paraphernalia of romance, illustrate in his visions the most abstract theological ideas. He tells us that " his desire was to become and be called a Servitor of the Eternal Wisdom "—yet he conceived of this attribute of Deity almost in the manner of chivalry as " a gentle loving Mistress, rich in wisdom and overflowing with love."

Thus it grew into a habit with him, whenever he heard songs of praise, or the sweet music of stringed instruments, or lays, or discourse about earthly love, immediately to turn his heart and mind inwards, and gaze abstractedly upon his loveliest Love, whence all love flows. It were impossible to tell how often with weeping eyes, from out the unfathomable depth of his outspread heart, he embraced this lovely form, and pressed it tenderly to his heart. And thus it fared with him as with a sucking child, which lies encircled by its mother's arms upon her breast. As the child with its head and the movement of its body lifts itself up against its tender mother, and by these loving gestures testifies its heart's delight, even so his heart many a time leapt up within his body towards the delightful presence of the Eternal Wisdom, and melted away in sensible affections.

Though in such visions as these we seem to see Suso's starved human affections seeking an outlet, the spiritual life was not for him chiefly a matter of ecstasies, visions and emotional consolations. Side by side with these, he practised a severe and indeed savage asceticism, which is described in his *Life* with horrifying detail. The Friends of God accepted in full the mediæval theory of physical penance, and Suso's vehement nature seized eagerly upon this opportunity of suffering for the sake of love. His self-inflicted torments lasted for over twenty years.

After this he was inwardly warned that the time of deliberate and exterior suffering was over. "All these practices were nothing more than a good beginning, and a breaking through his uncrushed natural man." He was now called to that Upper School of Perfect Resignation, in which the hard lesson of complete spiritual detachment was taught; a cardinal doctrine among the Friends of God, whose ideal of the mystical life was heroic and austere. The reluctance with which Suso, now worn with penances and approaching middle-age, faced this new call on his endurance, his openly expressed preference for a "comfortable life," and the stages by which he reached the heights of self-abandonment, are all set out with the simplicity and candour which make his autobiography one of the most precious and engaging documents in the whole range of mediæval mysticism. Exterior and interior trials seemed to gather round the unfortunate Servitor of the Eternal Wisdom; his noblest acts of charity brought scandal on his convent and himself; for years he was beset by temptations to doubt and despair, and was successively accused of hypocrisy, heresy and immorality.

During this time he lived in much seclusion ; but after eight years was inwardly taught that schooling was over and he must now " go forth to his neighbour." Though his gentle and sensitive nature was not adapted to popular success, and he never rivalled Tauler's eminence as a preacher, Suso's fervour and depth of spirituality were recognized ; and during the last period of his life many spiritual children gathered round him. He also restored many relaxed nunneries to a more strict religious observance, and became a beloved and successful director of souls. One of his spiritual daughters, the Swiss nun Elizabeth Stäglin, was evidently the chief joy and interest of his later years ; and his correspondence with her, which fills the last half of his *Life*, shows how beautiful was the link which bound together the scattered Friends of God. Elizabeth was an educated and intelligent girl, " of an angelic disposition within," who had studied the writings of Eckhart and found in them " a great many deep intellectual views very pleasant to reflect upon." Nevertheless she was conscious that these took her somewhat out of her depth, and wrote for help to Suso; asking him, with a pleasant touch of youthful conceit, to " pass over the common ordinary kind of instruction and deal with high subjects."

Suso's reply is that of the experienced man of prayer, who has reached the realities of spiritual life :

What I have to say will need but few words. True bliss lies not in beautiful words but good works. . . . Let alone for the present these deep questions and attend to those fit for thee. Thou seemest to me as yet a young unexercised sister, and therefore it will be more profitable to thee to hear about the first beginnings of the spiritual life.

Elizabeth showed her quality by accepting this snub meekly. She answered: " What I long for is not wise words, but a holy life . . . begin first with the lowest things and guide me in them, just as a school child is first taught what is fit for its young age."

Suso therefore told her bit by bit " the way in which he broke through created things to arrive at God," though he forbade his pupil to imitate his own methods in the matter of physical penance. " Seek not to imitate the severe exercises of thy spiritual father. . . . God has many kinds of crosses with which He chastens His friends. I look for Him to lay another sort of cross on thy shoulders." Under these wise and gentle counsels, Elizabeth progressed in the mystical life, and became capable of receiving from her director, who was plainly delighted by her theological enthusiasm, much high teaching based on " the holy Master Eckhart " and those " bright lights " St. Denis (the Areopagite) and " the dear St. Thomas." But the scholastic severity of his favourite authorities is softened and coloured by Suso's lovely and poetic mind. Thus when the maiden asks, " What is God ? " he first replies with a dreadful exactitude that He is " substantial Being," but his pupil upon this asking him to " tell her more about it," he bursts into a beautiful rhapsody on God as found in His creation, in which the artist and lover of all beauty conquers at least for a moment the scholar and ascetic :

GERMAN AND FLEMISH MYSTICISM

Look above thee and around thee to the four quarters of the universe, and see how wide and high the beautiful heaven is in its swift course, and how nobly its Master has adorned it with the seven planets, each of which, not to reckon in the moon, is much bigger than the whole earth, and how He has decked it with the countless multitude of the bright stars. Oh ! when in summer time the beautiful sun bursts forth unclouded and serene, what fruitfulness and blessings it bestows unceasingly upon the earth ! See how the leaves and grass shoot up, and the lovely flowers smile ; how forest, heath, and meadow ring again with the sweet song of nightingales and other little birds ; how all those little creatures, which stern winter had shut up, issue forth rejoicing, and pair together ; and how men too, both young and old, entranced with joy, disport themselves right merrily. Ah, gentle God, if Thou art so lovely in Thy creatures, how exceeding beautiful and ravishing Thou must be in Thyself ! But look again, I pray thee, and behold the four elements—earth, water, air, and fire, with all the wondrous things which they contain in manifold variety—men, beasts, birds, fishes and sea-monsters ; and mark how they all cry aloud together, Praise and honour be to the unfathomable immensity that is in Thee ! Who is it, Lord, that sustains all this ? Who feeds it all ? It is Thou who providest for all, each in its own way ; for great and small, for rich and poor. It is Thou, O God, who doest this. Thou, O God, art God indeed !

Come, daughter, thou hast now found thy God, whom thy heart has so long sought after. Look upwards, then, with sparkling eyes and radiant face and bounding heart, and behold Him and embrace Him with the infinite outstretched arms of thy soul and thy affection, and give thanks and praise to Him, the noble Prince of all creatures. See how, by gazing on this mirror, there springs up speedily, in a soul susceptible of such impressions, an intense inward jubilee ; for by jubilee is meant a joy which no tongue can tell, but which pours itself with might through heart and soul.

The chapters in which these communications are recorded witness to the lofty intellectual standard reached amongst the Friends of God, disproving the idea that they were merely a society of simple pietists or excited visionaries. Their mystical religion rested upon solid foundations, expressing itself not only in great purity of life, but in vigorous apostolic action. Elizabeth Stäglin died five years before her spiritual father. His *Life* ends with the vision of her liberated soul " shining with a dazzling brightness and full of a heavenly joy."

Contemporary with Suso and Tauler, and influenced by their doctrines, though hardly to be reckoned amongst the formal adherents of the Friends of God, was one of the greatest—perhaps the very greatest—of the mystics of the Church. John Ruysbroeck (1293–1381), brought up in Brussels by two learned and holy priests, and accustomed from childhood to the atmosphere of spiritual religion, spent the first half of his life as a chaplain of the cathedral of St. Gudule. Simple and unassuming, going about his ordinary business with " a mind lifted up into God," he seems to have moved gently and without crisis to the heights of the contemplative life. When he was fifty years old, the longing for greater solitude and quiet drove him from the city. With his two foster-fathers he left Brussels and established at Groenendael, in the forest of Soignes, a small community under the Augustinian rule. Here he lived peacefully for thirty-eight years, and here he wrote his greatest mystical works.

Ruysbroeck's teaching cannot be summarized. No words other than his own can suggest its real quality, for it implies and proceeds from an experience of God which transcends the normal process of the mind. It has that peculiar character which great mystical literature shares with great poetry ; with each fresh reading it discloses fresh truths and secrets to those—and only those—

who are ready to receive them. Increased familiarity with these writings brings a growing conviction that a real weight of meaning must be attached to every phrase, and that those which seem obscure to us are dark with excess of light. Ruysbroeck is struggling to describe a genuine experience of Reality, so great when measured by our common human level, that the effort to understand him, to follow his enraptured ascent to " that wayless being which all interior spirits have chosen above all other things," leaves us bewildered and awed.

Yet a certain method, borrowed in part from earlier writers—though only so borrowed, we may be sure, because experience had proved its worth —can be discerned in his works ; and a knowledge of this method helps us to understand him. He always treats the spiritual life as a growth or progress. It begins on simple human levels, with the purifying and ordering of that natural life of the senses which, with all its animal impulses and inevitable moral struggles, must yet be the raw material of sanctity.

The first business of " those who follow the way of Love " is to " be like other good people," in fulfilling the duties of outward or " active " life. They must renounce self-will, learn to bear provocation with gentleness, show a friendly face, and be ready to serve, give, and lend to everyone, while cleaving to God alone. Moreover they must be faithful to the ordinances of the Church ; for Ruysbroeck, the most transcendental of all mystics, highly valued corporate and sacramental religion. Only those whose will and senses have been thus disciplined and mortified are fit for the next stage :

that interior life in which the reason in its turn is sublimated, " nourished and fulfilled by the Spirit," and receives the supersensual illumination which " is not God, but is the light whereby we perceive Him." Beyond this again is the true contemplative or " super-essential " life of the God-desiring soul—" above reason, but not without reason "— wherein the spirit is lifted up " according to a way that is wayless," and lives in God and God in it.

There are we emptied of ourselves and of every creature, and made one with God in love. But between us and God this unity for ever ceaselessly renews itself; for the Spirit of God, outflowing and indrawing, touches and stirs our spirit, urging us to live according to the beloved will of God, and love Him as He deserveth . . . as God sendeth us forth, with all His gifts, to live according to His beloved will, so His Spirit draweth us within, to love Him as He deserveth.

Thus for Ruysbroeck the " supreme summit of the inner life " is not an achieved condition of still beatitude, a blank absorption in the Absolute ; it is, on the contrary, a life so rich and so abundant that it requires for its expression the extremes of activity and of rest, pouring itself out in generous acts of charity to " all in common," and yet " inwardly abiding in unbroken repose." In this it is the faint copy of that Divine life and love which the mystic " perceives in his inward seeing," as a common good pouring forth through heaven and earth, and drawing all things to itself, yet which is " eternally still and wayless according to the simplicity of its Essence."

In language directly borrowed from Eckhart, Ruysbroeck identifies the Divine activity in which every soul must share with " the Trinity of the Persons of God " ; and the eternal repose tasted in contemplation with the Godhead or Simple Being. But these expressions, when he employs them, lose their dry and abstract character and become transfused with life and love. No other mystic gives to his readers so deep a sense of unsearchable mystery, yet of almost intolerable joys. To do this he needed, and used, all that the intellectualism of the Early and Middle Ages—in Augustine, Dionysius, Richard of St. Victor, Eckhart, and Aquinas—could give him; and by its means conveys to us at least a hint of ineffable adventures, together with the certitude that " all we taste, against all we lack, is like a single drop of water against the whole sea . . . for we feed upon His Immensity, which we cannot devour, and we yearn after His Infinity, which we cannot attain."

ILLUSTRATIVE WORKS

Eckhart, Meister. Translated by C. de B. Evans. London, 1924.

Inge, W. R. Christian Mysticism. 2nd ed. London, 1912.

Jones, Rufus. Studies in Mystical Religion. London,1909.

Ruysbroeck. The Adornment of the Spiritual Marriage, The Book of Truth, The Sparkling Stone. Translated by P. Wynschenk Dom. London, 1916.

The XII Béguines. Translated by J. Francis. London, 1913.

Suso. Life. Translated by T. F. Knox. London, 1913.

The Little Book of Eternal Wisdom. London, 1910.

Tauler, John. Twenty-five Sermons. Translated by S. Winkworth. New edition. London, 1906.

The Inner Way : Thirty-six Sermons for Festivals. 3rd edition. London, 1909.

Theologia Germanica. Edited by S. Winkworth. London, 1907.

Underhill, E. Ruysbroeck. London, 1915.

CHAPTER VIII

THE TWO CATHERINES

ST. CATHERINE OF SIENA—ST. CATHERINE OF GENOA

THE last splendours of the mediæval period and the
transition to the Renaissance—terms in a sense
conventional, but nevertheless indicating genuine
historic facts—are summed up in the domain of
the spiritual life in the careers of two great women.
Both Italians, born exactly a century apart, St.
Catherine of Siena (1347–80), the contemporary
of Ruysbroeck and Julian of Norwich, and St.
Catherine of Genoa (1447–1510), at whose death
St. Ignatius, the hero of the counter-reformation,
was just nineteen years old, stand up among a
crowd of men and women of lesser spiritual genius as
supreme representatives of the energy and originality
of the Christian mystical type. I do not apologize
for devoting a chapter to these classic figures, whose
achievement gives so many clues to the true nature
and meaning of the contemplative life.

Catherine of Siena was born at a time of almost
unequalled ecclesiastical degradation. We know
this, not from Protestant critics, but from the
terrible words in which she and other Catholic
saints of the fourteenth century have described the
clerical corruption which they saw. Politically,
too, Italy was full of internal wars, treachery,

miseries of every kind. Yet in this period of violence, wickedness and suffering, the life of the spirit burned with a peculiar intensity; and much in Catherine's surroundings fed and developed her genius. In vivid contrast to the state of the official Church, with the Papacy at Avignon, and sins and abuses of every kind flourishing almost unchecked, was the network of mystical devotion—mostly propagated by groups of lay-folk gathered round some saintly character—which had spread over Western Europe and attracted to itself all fervent spirits. In Germany, during her childhood, the movement of the Friends of God was at its height ; in England the followers of Rolle continued his work ; in Italy Giovanni Columbini, a rich Sienese merchant who had embraced utter poverty, was founding the congregation of the Gesuati, which sought to revive the simplicity and ardour of St. Francis, and caused a considerable reformation among the friars ; whilst St. Bridget of Sweden (1303–73), a mystic of the type of St. Hildegarde, was pouring forth apocalyptic prophecies and political denunciations at Rome.

Into this world of mingled ferocity and beauty Catherine, a child of genius, was born in 1347. Her father was a prosperous householder in the tanners' quarter of Siena ; she was among the youngest of a large family. Even as a child, Catherine, like Hildegarde and other mystics, is said to have received vivid religious impressions. The visionary world of imaginative children took with her a spiritual form. Her precocity was extraordinary. Before she was sixteen, she had determined to consecrate her life to God. At this age she took the habit of the Sisters of Penance of St. Dominic—pious women who followed a religious rule in their own homes—and lived in entire seclusion in one little room in her father's house; devoting herself to prayer and practising a severe asceticism. Under the influence of this existence, with its total concentration on the inner life, her mystical powers developed quickly ; and this, the first or educative phase of her career, was completed before she was twenty. It was marked not only by numerous ecstasies and visions, and terrible battles with " evil spirits," which some will attribute to unnatural repression of her temperament and others to her vivid consciousness of sin; but also by the steady expansion of her remarkable spiritual faculties. This period culminated in the experience known as her " Mystical Marriage with Christ " in 1366 : a dramatic vision which doubtless owed something to the lovely legend of her namesake, St. Catherine of Alexandria. It marked a real epoch in the development of Catherine Benincasa's soul : her transition from a purely ecstatic and personal to an active and altruistic mysticism. In after life she realized that this period of solitary absorption in God had been a means of attaining that utter penetration by the Divine love and will in which she afterwards performed her public work.

In obedience to the Divine Voice, which told her that it was time to pass on to other souls the grace and certitude she had received, she now left her cell; and devoted herself first to the sick poor of Siena, nursing, comforting and converting. Often her tranquil and unselfish presence healed the illness whilst it pacified the soul. She was ready for any menial employment, and in all ways exhibited the truth of her own great maxim, that "there is no perfect virtue—none that bears fruit—unless it is exercised by means of our neighbour." Gradually her spiritual force became recognized, and a circle—including not only devoted women, but learned friars and priests and wild young nobles—gathered round her, for whom this young girl was "our Holy Mother," and over whom she exercised an unquestioned authority. To these she taught, with the calm yet humble certitude of one who knows herself to be in touch with deep sources of life and truth, her doctrine of self-knowledge and of the Cross. She read their hearts, turned them from evil, trained them in the spiritual life, and herself did penance for their sins. The power of human character has seldom been more strikingly exhibited.

Doubtless Catherine obtained from her Dominican followers—especially from the close friend of her later years, the erudite and spiritual Fra Raimondo—the many theological conceptions and images which she employed in her teaching ; but the intellectual grasp displayed in her use of them, and the fire and life with which she filled them, were her own. Her intuition, both in heavenly and earthly things, was apparently unerring ; and there is evidence that, like so many of the great mystics, she possessed a certain clairvoyant faculty, often being exactly aware of the thoughts and deeds of her absent "children," and especially of their temptations and falls. Thus Francesco Malavolti, whom she had converted and brought " from being a bestial and wellnigh devilish man to true knowledge and life," states in his depositions that, having once fallen back into a secret sin "known only to God," Catherine immediately divined it, and urged him to confession :

> And when I sought some delay, refusing to do it just then, she, with a glowing and kindling countenance, said to me : "How, my son, dost thou think that I have not mine eyes ever open over my children ? Thou couldst not do or say anything without my knowing it. And how dost thou think to hide from me that thou hast just now done so and so ? Go therefore immediately and cleanse thyself from such great misery." Then, when I heard her tell me precisely all that I had done and said, confused and shameful, and without other answer, at once and heedfully I fulfilled her command.

This picture of the lawless young aristocrat dominated and forced to repentance by a girl of the people, probably his junior in age, gives us already a hint of the strength which made Catherine one of the most amazing figures in the history of Christian mysticism; and helps us to understand her declaration that her one desire had been "to know and follow the Truth in a more *virile* way." But strength was not the only source of her power ; her great personal charm can still be felt in her letters and in the many touching stories of the love she inspired. Although her naturally good health had been injured by austerities and she was often ill, those who knew her said that she was "always merry and happy"; for she had not been afraid to ask that she might bear "all the pains and infirmities there are in the world" in her own body if thus she might contribute to its redemption, and every additional suffering thus became a joy. During this, the middle period of her life, her ecstasies and visions were frequent. They reached their culmination in 1370, in a trance which lasted four hours. Her friends supposed her dead, and Catherine herself always held that her spirit had indeed left the body and entered into eternal life, but was sent back again to earth to minister to other souls.

> Because my soul shrank with horror from this return, the Lord said to me, " The salvation of many souls demands thy return, and thou shalt no more live as thou hast lived hitherto, nor have henceforth thy cell for habitation, but shalt go out from thine own city for the good of souls. I shall be ever with thee, and shall guide thee and bring thee back. Thou shalt bear the honour of My name and witness to spiritual things before small and great, layfolk, clergy and religious ; and I shall give thee words and wisdom none shall be able to withstand."

This crucial experience marks the beginning of Catherine's real public career. Always intensely though dimly conscious of vocation, with the development of her immense genius for prayer the nature of this vocation now became clear to her. She was twenty-three, and had before her only ten years of life. They were spent in activities, partly political and partly apostolic, for which nothing in her birth and scanty education seemed to prepare her. We shall hardly realize the bearing of these activities unless we perceive how profoundly spiritual, yet how sternly practical, was Catherine's conception of the nature of that Church which she so passionately loved. To her the Pope really was, or should be, that which she so often named him, " Our sweet father, Christ on earth " ; and she looked persistently for such a return of Christian power and purity to the spiritual rulers of Christendom that " what God now permits by force shall be accomplished by love." Possessed by this vision, she was faced by the spectacle of the fourteenth-century Papacy, given over to ignoble politics, hiring mercenary troops to make war upon its own spiritual children, and driving the chief Italian communes into open hostility to the Church ; the priesthood full of corruption, the Pope in exile at Avignon, the Cardinals thinking of anything rather than the good of souls and the purposes of God.

To Catherine, one of the most thoroughly institutional and yet profoundly transcendental of all the mystics of the Church, it seemed clear that those purposes must require the making of peace with the insurgent Italian cities and the bringing back of the Papacy to Rome; the restoration of religious discipline and purity. As her influence and reputation for holiness spread, she devoted them to these objects. She wrote, through her secretaries, innumerable letters—of which over four hundred have been preserved—to persons of every sort ; and travelled as unofficial diplomatist through Italy and to Avignon itself, as the almost dictatorial adviser and representative of the chief political personages of the time. Her one desire was to bring about a peace in which the Christian life could flourish and the spiritual authority of the Church be restored ; and there can be little doubt that hers was the decisive influence which brought Gregory XI back to Rome.

"Answer the summons of God !" she wrote to him, "Who is calling you to come, hold, and possess the place of the glorious shepherd St. Peter, whose vicar you are. Lift up the banner of the holy Cross. Come, that you may reform the Church with good shepherds, giving back to her the colour of most ardent charity that she has lost ; for so much blood has been sucked from her by wicked devourers that she is pale. But take heart, and come, Father ! Do not make the servants of God wait, who are afflicted in longing. And I, poor wretched woman, can wait no more ; living, I seem to die in pain, as seeing God thus outraged !"

Yet the remarkable ascendancy which is displayed in such letters, and which made Catherine for a few years one of the chief political personages of her time, was exercised with the deep humility of one who knew herself the unworthy agent of another Power. She used it always and wholly for the good of souls. " I came," she said in answer to some complaint laid against her, " for nought else save to eat and taste souls and draw them from the hands of the devils. For this I would lay down my life if I had a thousand, and for this I shall go or stay, as the Holy Spirit shall direct." Political action never reduced her passionate interest in, and care for, her spiritual family —now greatly increased in numbers—or her devotion to apostolic work among the poor. So many were the conversions she effected that she was called with justice " the mother of thousands of souls." During the last years of her life, wherever she appeared, people flocked to her, and were often brought to repentance merely by the sight of her face. Yet she remained meekly conscious of her own imperfections, always lived a life of penance —for her vivid sense of Christian unity involved the mystery of vicarious suffering—and charged to her own sins every failure in the success of her mission. Worn out by a compelling power and passion too strong for her frail physical health, she died at Rome in 1380, aged only thirty-three.

If it is Catherine's amazing public ministry which first strikes the imagination, this only represents one aspect of her greatness. It was the temporal expression of something reaching far beyond itself : the profound experience of God and consequent sense of vocation, which began at adolescence and persisted throughout her life, often overwhelming her by its intensity, and producing the so-called mystical, but really psychological, states of rapture and ecstasy. Though all that St. Catherine was able to report of the truths learnt in these deep absorptions was a fragment of the whole, it was enough to give her a great place among the teaching mystics. Like other women contemplatives of the first rank—St. Hildegarde, Angela of Foligno, and her contemporary Julian of Norwich—she combined with an ardent spirituality remarkable intellectual power. Her chief literary work, the *Divine Dialogue*, largely consists in an account of the direct teaching she received from God in her ecstasies and contemplations, with the results of her own meditations thereon : in this closely resembling the *Revelations* of Julian of Norwich. It is said to have been dictated "in a state of ecstasy"; but this probably means little more than that deep, brooding concentration in which the surface faculties are in abeyance, and the "spiritual seeing and hearing" have possession of the mental field.

The *Dialogue* gives ample evidence of deep, clear thinking and of wide acquaintance with the language and concepts of theology. We find in it practical counsels and unmeasured denunciation of clerical vices, alternating with passages of marvellous beauty, which take us into those regions beyond thought where Catherine declares that she has beheld " the hidden things of God," and " tasted and seen with the light of the intellect in Thy Light the Abyss of Thine Eternal Trinity and the beauty of Thy creatures." It is not the mere emotional outpouring of a fervent visionary, but the solemn testament of a soul which has been raised to such a contemplation of supernatural truth that she is able to say of it, "The more I enter, the more I find, and the more I find the more I seek of Thee. Thou art the Food that never satiates, for when the soul is satiated in Thine abyss it is not satiated, but ever continues to hunger and thirst for Thee." The Truth is one of Catherine's favourite names for Christ ; and her test of spiritual health is the soul's ever-growing capacity for seeing things as they really are. Thus she writes to the Bishop of Castello " with the desire of seeing you illuminated with a true and perfect light " ; and this true and perfect light is identical with that self-knowledge in which she taught her disciples to live as in a cell. It is not a niggling introspection, but that clear view of human nothingness matched against the perfection of God which is the sovereign remedy against pride and self-love ; the only foundation of that charity which she calls in one of her jewelled phrases " a continual prayer."

The soul is a tree existing by love, and can live by nothing else but love. If this soul have not in truth the divine love of perfect Charity she cannot produce the fruit of life, but only of death.

Needs be then that the root of this tree, that is the affection of the soul, should grow in and issue from the circle of true self-knowledge which is contained in Me, who have neither beginning nor end, like the circumference of a circle. For turn as thou wilt within a circle, inasmuch as the circumference has no end nor beginning, thou always remainest within it. And this knowledge of thyself and of Me is found in the earth of true humility, which is as wide as the diameter of the circle, that is, the knowledge of self and of Me.

Catherine of Siena's great namesake, Caterina Adorna—afterwards known as St. Catherine of Genoa—was born in 1447. Externally, the circumstances and character of these two mystics differed widely, yet they had in common several important qualities and convictions. The first was a girl of the people, of ardently spiritual temperament, who gave herself to God when little more than a child, and never wavered from her allegiance. Her mysticism was intensely visionary and Christocentric ; the public career which it inspired almost sensational in character. The second was an aristocrat, whose naturally hypersensitive and melancholy disposition had been aggravated by an unhappy marriage, and whose conversion at the age of twenty-six was at least in part the result of disillusionment. Her mysticism at its full development had a deeply philosophic side ; she had few visions ; her public work was that of a devoted and clear-sighted philanthropist. In both the tendency to mystical absorption in God was balanced by a powerful intellect, by a passion for active and apostolic work, and by a sacramental sense which found expression in intense devotion to the Eucharist—for them the focal point of external religion. Thus they stand together as examples of the proper co-ordination of every part of a full human personality; its complete consecration to the purposes of the Spirit. Both were able to express in words at least something of the truths which they had realized, and left behind them teaching which, had it come from a trained theologian, would still have been remarkable for its authority, originality, and depth. Both gathered and held a group of devoted disciples, to whom they gave something of their own spiritual fire.

Catherine of Genoa was abruptly aroused from religious indifference and deep melancholy by an experience in which " her heart was pierced by so sudden and immense a love of God, accompanied by so deep a sight of her miseries and sins and of His Goodness, that she was near falling to the ground; and in a transport of pure and all-purifying love she was drawn away from the miseries of the world." This happened in 1474. She at once gave herself to work among the sick poor, deliberately undertaking the most repulsive duties, in order to cure her natural fastidiousness. For four years she combined this persevering life of active detailed charity with a penitential discipline chiefly directed towards the mortification of the will. She gave many hours daily to prayer, and practised severe austerities; as most contemplatives of the Catholic type have felt impelled to do during their first period of education.

The expansion and consecration of her great abilities followed naturally on this sacrifice of personal enjoyments. In 1477 she founded the first hospital in Genoa. It soon became her permanent home and principal sphere of activity;

and from this time onwards her life was a perfect illustration of St. Teresa's maxim that " to give our Lord a perfect service Martha and Mary must combine."

Her penitential phase was now over ; and during the central period of her life, from about 1477 to 1499—when she was fifty-two years old— she lived in the almost unbroken consciousness of the Divine presence ; a consciousness which inundated her with love and joy, and often caused ecstasies from which she is said to have come forth " happy and rosy-faced." Yet during the same period she managed with skill and devotion the affairs of the hospital. Her accounts were never a farthing wrong, nor was she ever known to fail in her duties through absorption in spiritual joys. When the plague came to Genoa, she was the centre of a devoted band who went through the city nursing the victims, and in many cases sacrificed their own lives.

It is when we balance the height achieved in her mystical contemplation by the width and ardour of this outflowing love and compassion—a compassion which passed beyond humanity to all creatures, so that " if an animal were killed or a tree cut down, she could hardly bear to see them lose the being God had given "—that we begin to realize the greatness of Catherine's soul. She fully satisfied the demand of Ruysbroeck, that the " truly inward man should flow out to all in common." " Thou dost command me to love my neighbour," she once exclaimed in prayer, " and yet I cannot love anything but Thee, nor can I admit anything else to be mingled with

Thee. How then can I act?" And she was
answered inwardly : "He who loves Me, loves
all that I love." Her influence gradually spread ;
and, perhaps in unconscious imitation of her great
namesake of Siena, she gathered round her one
of those spiritual groups which seem so congenial
to the Italian religious temper. It was in conversation with these disciples, and mostly in the eight
years between 1499 and 1507—when her health
finally broke down—that her great mystical doctrines were developed and expressed.

Catherine's earliest biographer testifies to the
moving character of these conferences, when " each
fed on spiritual food of a delicious kind, and because
time fled so quickly could never be satiated; but,
all burning within, would remain there unable at
last to speak, unable to depart, as though in
ecstasy !" Some of her sayings of this period are
among the strangest which the Christian mystics
have left to us, and seem almost to imply the
claim to an actual transmutation of her personality;
that which is known in mystical theology as
the " transforming union " of the soul with God.
" My *me* is God, nor do I know my selfhood, save
in Him !" " My being is God, not by simple
participation but by a true transformation of my
being." " God is my being, my self, my strength,
my blessedness !" In the development which
was crowned by such convictions as these, we have
an almost classical example of spiritual growth;
moving out from the limitations of a selfish and
unsatisfied naturalism, through purifying self-discipline and service, to the levels of full, creative
personality.

THE MYSTICS OF THE CHURCH

St. Catherine of Genoa stands almost alone among the great Catholic women mystics, on account of the naturally Platonic bent of her mind. Deeply influenced by the writings of Dionysius the Areopagite and the poems of Jacopone da Todi, she conceived of eternal things most easily under great abstract images, and seldom used the language of personality. Not Christ, but the Infinite God, is the centre of her devotion ; and were it not for her intense love of the Eucharist—bringing this unmeasured Reality to a personal focus—we might call her mysticism less Christian than theistic. God is for her Light, Fire, Love ; a living, all-pervading, peaceful Ocean of Reality. " Pure Love is no other than God." " Love, I want Thee, the whole of Thee." " Wouldst thou that I should show thee what thing God is ? Peace ; that peace which no man finds, who departs from Him." " I am so placed and submerged in His immense love, that I seem as though immersed in the sea, and nowhere able to touch, see or feel aught but water."

Her deep and beautiful doctrine concerning the soul's purification after death, by which perhaps she is now best known, is wholly based on this conception of the perfected harmony between human and Divine love, as the essential constituent of all full life. God and the soul, the two supreme spiritual realities, are here placed over against each other ; and the inevitable suffering which is endured by each imperfect spirit in the course of its purification originates in the bitter realization of this its own separation from the Divine will and love. Yet this is a happy suffering, full of hope, and willingly, even eagerly, embraced; for it is caused by the creature's capacity for God, and leads to its fulfilment in Him. " It consumes in the soul every imperfection. And, when the soul is thus purified, it abides all in God, without any thing of its own." Here, in this consummation of Catherine's doctrine, that close alliance between the ethical and the mystical which is characteristic of all that is best in Christian spirituality, achieves triumphant expression.

ILLUSTRATIVE WORKS

Catherine of Genoa, St. The Treatise on Purgatory. London, 1858.

Catherine of Siena, St. Divine Dialogue. Translated by Algar Thorold. London, 1896.

Letters. Translated by V. D. Scudder. London, 1905.

Gardner, Edmund. St. Catherine of Siena. London, 1907.

Hügel, Baron F. von. The Mystical Element of Religion as Studied in St. Catherine of Genoa and her Friends. 2nd edition. 2 vols. London, 1923.

CHAPTER IX

SPANISH MYSTICISM

ST. IGNATIUS LOYOLA—ST. PETER OF ALCANTARA—
ST. TERESA—ST. JOHN OF THE CROSS

THE great Spanish mystics form a compact group,
all living and writing within the sixteenth century
and mostly in close connection with the religious
orders of St. Augustine, St. Francis, and Mount
Carmel. Even the outstanding exception to this,
St. Ignatius Loyola, became a religious founder in
his turn. Thus they arise within the great stream
of Western Christianity, and the national and
personal character which many of them exhibit is
fully articulated to, and nourished by, the general
spiritual tradition of their day. They use the
language, and follow the classifications, to which
the mediæval mystics have accustomed us ; and
such diverse and exotic influences as the writings
of Tauler, Suso, and Ruysbroeck, and the poems of
Jacopone da Todi, are found to have affected them.
  If we wish to define the peculiar character of
Spanish spirituality, we shall find it perhaps in an
intensely austere, practical, indeed militant, temper;
an outlook on reality which leaves small space for
mere religious emotionalism ; a tendency, once
the principles of the spiritual life have been accepted,
to push them at all costs to their logical end.

" Naught is needful, save only God," says Juan de los Angeles. " By this," says St. John of the Cross, " may be known the soul which in truth loves God, if it is content with nothing save only God." And this, says St. Teresa, means, not devotional raptures, but the stern virtues of " humility, justice, and fortitude," since " our merit does not consist in enjoyment, but in work, in suffering and in love." " Let each one reflect," says St. Ignatius, " that just so much does he advance in all spiritual things, as he goes out from self-love, self-will, and self-interest " ; and Orozco adds, " He who would see the face of that most powerful Wrestler, our boundless God, must first have wrestled with himself."

This stern and bracing view of human character emerges again and again. St. Ignatius (1491–1556)—not always recognized, as he should be, as a true constructive mystic—is here typical of Spanish spirituality. The immense energies of his active life, the unlimited demands which he made upon himself and every soul that he trained, the calm disregard of difficulties and ill-health and consequent triumph over circumstances, the accompanying inward movement which transformed this fiery soldier and drastic evangelist into a saint who seemed to his companions " all love "—all these things combine to make the life of Ignatius one of the classics of heroic Christianity. We see in him the double movement of the mystic ; first the retirement and inward concentration of his life at Manresa, then the immense activity to which it led.

The *Spiritual Exercises*, which have had and still retain so immense an influence on the education

of souls, are—in spite of an outward appearance
of formalism—the true expression of this realistic
and devoted spirit. They are the work of a
mystic acutely conscious of the reality of God
and His overwhelming claim upon the soul. In
the words of Ignatius, their one object is " to
allow the Creator to work directly on the creature,
and the creature with her Creator and Lord." All
the machinery, the linked series of formal meditations, the numerous instructions, the carefully
graduated " points," are really cumulative and
exquisitely chosen suggestions, intended to help the
pupil to attain this first-hand communion for himself. The aim is accomplished with a precision
on which the modern psychologist could hardly
improve, and which none but a practical mystic
could achieve; whilst in the accompanying " colloquies," where the soul is taught to speak with
God " as a friend with a friend," we have the
experimental prayer of the born contemplative
applied with an extraordinary skill to the needs of
the ordinary man. Bit by bit this two-fold method
forces the soul to an ever clearer view of its own
nature and destiny, along a road which closely
follows the traditional " mystic way "—namely
through a compulsory and purifying self-knowledge
—to the " illuminated " state in which it is capable
of that crucial act of election on which the direction
of its growth is to depend; and so to the conclusion of the whole matter, " the achievement of
love divine." Through all we feel the drive and
determination of the soldier, whose natural attitude
is the attitude of attack, and who shirks nothing
and forgets nothing which can contribute to the

chosen end. It is a spiritual drill, directed to a definite result; but a drill which implies and rests on a profound and vivid understanding of the business of the soul.

Ignatius administered the *Exercises* to the simplest Christians as well as to the heroic members of his own company. It is largely due to their peculiar educative power that St. Teresa found in the Society of Jesus her first real helpers and advisers in the mystical life ; for already, before the death of St. Ignatius, his sons began to stand out above the average religious level, and were, as she tells us, " known as very experienced men in matters of spirituality." " These blessed men of the Society of Jesus," as she afterwards called them, remained during the greater part of her life her chief and best counsellors. She calls them prudent and strengthening—characteristics which she was well able to appreciate. Through them, the stern Ignatian spirit exercised a directly formative influence upon her ; and again through her on the countless souls who have learned in her books the practice of mystical devotion. It seems probable that her celebrated definition of mental prayer as " friendship with God " is ultimately derived from the Ignatian colloquies. Their military sobriety, appealing to the practical side of her character, balanced the fervours of St. Peter of Alcantara (1499–1562), who brings into the stream of Spanish mysticism the Franciscan enthusiasm and spirit of unbridled penance, and with whom she was intimate in the last four years of her life.

Had Peter of Alcantara, rather than the wise St. Francis Borgia and his associates, had the direction of St. Teresa's soul during the crucial period of its development, it is improbable that she would have lived to reform the Carmelite Order. But his ferocious and almost unbelievable asceticism, described in a celebrated chapter of her autobiography, was only one side of a life of great holiness and incessant labour devoted to the restoration in Spain of the primitive Franciscan Rule. His mystical works, intended purely for edification, mostly follow traditional lines. Neither his austerities nor his ecstatic contemplation, however, prevented him, as Teresa herself observes, from " being with all his sanctity very agreeable." The communion of spirit between them appears to have been very close : indeed, St. Teresa firmly believed that after his death he continued to advise and support her, and found him " a greater comfort than when he was on earth."

Formed in part by the Ignatian spirit and method, and receiving through St. Peter the influence of Franciscan mysticism, St. Teresa (1515–82) was also touched by all the other mystical forces and persons active in sixteenth-century Spain; so that any real account of Spanish mysticism must give to her the central place. She first learnt the art of meditation from the writings of the Franciscan friar Osuna (c. 1540) ; she corresponded with the Blessed John of Avila, the " Apostle of Andalusia " (1500–69), and a close acquaintance of the early Jesuits. St. John of the Cross (1542–91), one of the few supreme Christian contemplatives, was her devoted colleague and friend. The richness and charm of St. Teresa's character can still be felt in her works—more read, perhaps, than those of any other mystic. She is the classic example of that complete flowering of personality in which the life of contemplation does not tend to specialism, but supports and enhances a strenuous active career. To write a series of works which are at once among the glories of Spanish literature, and the best and most exact of guides to the mysteries of the inner life ; to practise, and describe with an unequalled realism, the highest degrees of prayer and contemplation ; to found numerous convents in the face of apparently insuperable difficulties ; to reform a great religious Order in spite of the opposition of those pious conservatives whom she was accustomed to call pussy-cats ; to control at once the financial and spiritual situations of her enterprise, and to do all this in spite of persistent ill-health in a spirit of unfailing common sense, of gaiety, of dedicated love—this, which is far from exhausting the list of St. Teresa's activities, seems a sufficient programme for one soul.

The chief events of her life are well known, and need only be given briefly here. A girl of the aristocratic class, romantic and ardent in temperament, fond of all activities, of pleasure and social intercourse, she was nevertheless drawn early to religion ; and became a novice in the Carmelite Convent of the Incarnation at Avila before she was twenty years of age. Four years later she fell seriously ill, was paralysed for two years, and emerged with her first spiritual ardour much reduced. For a time she gave up contemplative prayer, in which she had already made some progress, and acquiesced in the lax religious life of her convent. A struggle now began, and lasted for over twelve years, between Teresa's mystical vocation and her very human love of active life. This conflict testifies to the breadth and essential sanity of her mind, capable of a wide range of inward and outward interest and response. She has described vividly in the early chapters of her autobiography the alternations of her divided will, never able to give up the life of prayer and self-oblation, yet never willing entirely to capitulate to its imperious demands.

> On the one side God was calling me, on the other I was following the world. All the things of God gave me great pleasure, and I was a prisoner to the things of the world. It seemed as if I wished to reconcile two contradictions so much at variance with one another as are the life of the spirit and the joys, pleasures and amusements of sense. . . . I passed nearly twenty years on this stormy sea, falling and rising, but rising to no good purpose seeing that I went and fell again.

Her real state was hidden from her companions, who, seeing her love of helping souls, and her many acts of devotion, held her in special honour ; a fact which increased her shame and self-contempt. At last, with the beginning of middle-age, the struggle reached its term ; states of recollection and peace gradually began to predominate over the longing for outward distractions, and, as she says, her " prayer began to be solid like a house "—a truly Teresian phrase, bringing before us her profound distrust of emotional fancies, her craving for an unadorned reality.

Her forty-first year saw the end of the period of conflict ; and Teresa's full mystical life at last began. Prepared in the hiddenness during the purifying years of temptation, it developed swiftly.

In two years she had passed through those degrees
of prayer called " quiet " and " union," which are
so marvellously described in the *Life*, and reached
the heights of ecstatic contemplation. It is un-
necessary to describe the long series of " visions "
and " voices," the trances and states of rapturous
absorption which would now come upon her, even
in public, to her great distress ; and which at first
puzzled and alarmed her spiritual advisers. These
were simply the abnormal means by which an
exceptionally ardent and imaginative nature realized
and expressed its overwhelming experience of God.
St. Teresa's own frank and detailed account of
them, and of the tests by which she tried to avoid
delusion, is—thanks to her remarkable genius for
self-analysis—one of the most important psychological documents which we possess. It was at
this time that she was first helped by the sober
wisdom and experience of the early Jesuit fathers,
and the Ignatian spirituality made its great contribution to the developing mysticism of Spain.

The steady growth of her contemplative power
brought with it the inevitable longing for a life
of greater austerity and seclusion; impossible to
achieve in the Convent of the Incarnation, where
the nuns were unenclosed, and saw much of their
friends in the world. More and more the laxity
of the Rule displeased and distressed her, though
it was not until the year 1560 that she first realized
her call to found a convent in poverty, where the
life of self-denial might be fully lived. The active
and creative side of Teresa's character, in abeyance
during the first intense and largely educative years
of her mystical life, now again asserted itself, but

in complete subjection to her spiritual ideals. After great difficulty, she was able in 1562, when forty-seven years of age, to found the Convent of St. Joseph at Avila ; a small and poor house, where the primitive Rule of Mount Carmel was strictly observed.

This period of St. Teresa's career was also that of her fullest and most continuous mystical experience : which, far from interfering with her practical undertakings, illuminated and supported them from within. The very object of her soul's union with God was, as she said in a memorable passage, " Work ! work ! work ! " Her prayers, visions, and states of enraptured communion made her " more courageous and more free "; and gave her fresh energy and determination to deal with the obstacles which threatened again and again to wreck her enterprise.

In the very grievous trials, persecutions, and contradictions of these months, God gave me great courage ; and the more grievous they were, the greater the courage, without weariness in suffering.

That balanced and completed life of work and contemplation in which we seem to glimpse the sort of free response to the material and spiritual orders which awaits the maturity of man, was now hers. The spiritual and practical sides of her nature were completely harmonized. She could turn from directions about the finances of the community or the right sweeping down of the house, to deal in a manner equally wise and precise with the most delicate problems of the soul. Entirely given up from this time to the reforming and spiritualizing of the convents of her Order, and the educating of individual souls, St. Teresa is a classic example of the place which the mystic can and should fill in the life of the Church ; and completely answers the charges of spiritual selfishness and aloofness from practical problems sometimes brought against its contemplative saints. Indeed, it was often in physical hardships—the long journeys which she confesses she disliked, or the deprivation even of needful warmth and food— that she found the material of her inward joys.

We were (she says of her adventurous foundation of a convent in Toledo) for some days with no other furniture but two straw mattresses and one blanket, not even a withered leaf to fry a sardine with, till someone, I know not who, moved by our Lord, put a faggot in the church, with which we helped ourselves. At night it was cold, and we felt it. . . . The poverty we were in seemed to me as the source of a sweet contemplation.

The books through which her vivid spirit still reaches and affects us were written in the intervals of her many enterprises and journeys, as foundress and reformer of religious houses. Thanks to her innate literary power—for she ranks among the great prose writers of Spain—and to her frankness and psychological insight, these books, helped by her vivid and intimate letters of which a large number have been preserved, reveal Teresa's personality to us as few of the mystics have been revealed.

Two are autobiographical. The *Life*, dealing largely with her mystical experiences, was written at the wish of her directors. It brings the story of her development to the point at which she founded her first convent and began her active career, when she was about forty years old. This book, with its wonderfully clear and detailed account of the visionary and ecstatic phenomena which accompanied the education of her soul, has been ever since the *locus classicus* for those who desire to know what the higher degrees of mystical prayer, and the states of consciousness leading to and completed in ecstasy, feel like to those who experience them. The *Book of Foundations* deals with the ruling interests and events of her career as reformer and foundress; telling the story of the sixteen reformed convents of nuns which she established—often in circumstances of great difficulty—during the last fifteen years of her life. This work alone, so full of human interest and spiritual ardour, and abounding in examples of Teresian courage, wit, and common sense, is enough to establish her place among the great women of the Christian Church.

St. Teresa's other books contain the substance of her teaching on prayer and contemplation. *The Way of Perfection* was written for the sisters of St. Joseph's at Avila in the year 1566 ; *The Interior Castle*, her fullest and most orderly account of the spiritual life, in 1577. The brilliant and romantic girl, torn between the claims of two worlds, the exalted and courageous woman of prayer, with her unique combination of ecstasy and practicality, was now an experienced old nun. Physically worn out by ill-health, and the long and trying journeys undertaken for her reform, she had only five years to live. She was well versed in all the follies and self-deceptions of the religious temperament ; had borne persecution, misunderstanding, and obstruction from the ecclesiastical authorities, had known failure as well as success.   She knew all the exhaustion and desolations of the spiritual life, and the hard lot of the teacher who must often through her own interior darkness continue to help others toward the light.

> No foundation was made without trouble. . . . What it is to have to contend against many minds ! . . . Inwardly ill at ease, my soul was in very great dryness and darkness. . . . My health is generally weak, but I saw clearly that our Lord gives me strength. . . . I never refrained from making a foundation for fear of trouble, though I felt a great dislike to journeys, especially long ones. . . . It was my want of health that most frequently wearied me. . . . The weather was severe, and I, so old and sickly !

Phrases like these, scattered through the accounts of her superhuman activities, remind us of the ceaseless external tension within which her own spiritual life achieved maturity, and some of its greatest moments were experienced by her.   That life had indeed become one of constant and perfect intercourse with God—that deep and active union which some of the mystics have called the " spiritual marriage " or " transforming union " of the soul ; and which she herself describes in the last chapters of *The Interior Castle*.   Thus the difference between St. Teresa's first great book and her last, is the difference between the diary of the discoverer, and the considered instructions of the expert.   *The Interior Castle* teaches the gradual unfolding of the spiritual consciousness under the image of the successive habitations which the key of prayer unlocks for the soul.   It is full of Teresa's own bracing spirit ; her dislike of all pretensions, all seeking for consolations, all idle and dreamy enjoyments, all spiritual conceit.

The soul must be virile, not like those soldiers who lie down on their stomachs to drink when they are being led into battle. It must not dream of sweetness and enjoyments at the beginning of its career. Manna does not fall in the first habitations—we must press on further if we want to gather it ! Then alone will the soul find all things to its taste, when it has learned to will only that which God wills. How comic our pretensions are ! We are still immersed in difficulties and imperfections, we have virtues that can barely toddle, others hardly born ; and we are not ashamed to demand sweetness in prayer, we grumble at dryness ! May you never behave like that, sisters. Embrace the Cross—the rest is a mere extra. If God gives it you, thank Him meekly !

The very spirit of Spanish mysticism, militant, austere, practical, is in these words ; and this realistic and active conception of the soul's true business and God's true demand on it, which had steadily developed during the course of her own mystical life, now follows her even to the recesses of that " Seventh Habitation " where the divine union is achieved. For her that union means the total transfiguration of character : every power and aspect of the self enhanced, and dedicated to the redemptive purposes of God. She turns from the trances, ecstasies, visions, all that wealth of abnormal experiences which had accompanied the growth of her own soul. The ideal she now puts before her pupils is far indeed from that of the quietist.

What is the good, my daughters, of being deeply recollected in solitude, and multiplying acts of love, and promising our Lord to do wonders in His service, if, when we come out of our prayer, the least thing makes us do the exact opposite ? . . . The repose which those souls enjoy whom I speak of now is inward only; they have, and desire to have, less outwardly. For to what end, do you think, the soul sends from this Seventh Habitation, and as it were from her very deeps, aspirations into all the other habitations of this spiritual castle ? Do you think these messages to faculties, senses and body, have no other end but to invite them to sleep ? No, no, no ! Rather to employ them more than ever. . . . Moreover, the company the soul now enjoys gives her a strength she never had before. If, as David says, one becomes holy with the holy, who can doubt that this soul, who is now become *one thing* with the Mighty God by this high union of spirit with Spirit, shares His strength ? It is hence that the saints have drawn that courage which made them capable of suffering and dying for their God.

St. Teresa's friend and fellow-worker, the fragile and ardent little friar now known as St. John of the Cross (1542–91) exhibits at their best these intrepid, austere, realistic characteristics of Spanish mysticism on which she never ceased to lay stress. No other contemplative equals his power of bringing us face to face with the stark realities of the spiritual life ; the one aim set before it, and the price it demands. No other gives us an ideal of love at once so infinitely gentle, so supernatural, and so stern. Though his writing is didactic and impersonal, he leaves us in no doubt that personal experience of the most intense kind lies behind it ; and that he has himself proved the truth of his own maxim : " God values one effort of our own more than many of others on our behalf."

His original endowments differed widely from those of Teresa. She was an aristocrat ; he, of peasant origin. She was as much drawn to practical and organizing activities as to contemplation ; he, a natural ascetic and poet, was plainly happiest when " in secret where by none might I be spied ! " In her works we have the result of a fresh and deep personal experience, backed by Jesuit training and some study of Franciscan teachings upon prayer : in his, ardent experience is the basis too, but it is veiled under an impersonal form of presentation, and supported by theological training. The ecstatic soul is here seen through the professional mind. Entering the unreformed Carmelite Order in 1563 when he was twenty-one, St. John could not satisfy in it his longing for an austere and hidden life. He therefore thought of becoming a Carthusian monk ; but before he could put this plan into effect, he met St. Teresa, then a woman of fifty-two and at the height of her career as reformer and foundress. She was about to establish two houses of reformed friars ; and persuaded John of the Cross, whose quality she recognized, to undertake one of them. With two companions he established the first house, or rather hovel, of discalced Carmelite brothers, where a life of great saintliness and considerable squalor was led. Afterwards removing to Avila, he was for some years in close and constant touch with St. Teresa ; acting as her confessor, and also undertaking, with bracing results, the spiritual direction of her old Convent of the Incarnation, to which she had been sent as prioress. All St. Teresa's books were well known by him before the composition of his own works, which frequently betray their influence.

In 1577, the year in which *The Interior Castle* was finished, the opposition of the " unreformed " Carmelites to the rapid spread of the reforming movement came to a head. John of the Cross was captured by the conservative party, and imprisoned for eight months under barbarous conditions in a cell at Toledo. It was during this time of solitary incarceration, when the distractions of external life were in abeyance, that he experienced those raptures of divine union, " the most supreme delight of which the soul is capable in this life," which he tried later to analyse and explain in his mystical works. It was then, too, that he composed his great poems, *A Spiritual Canticle*, a paraphrase of parts of the Song of Solomon treating of the union between God and the Soul, and the lovely *In an Obscure Night*—poems which are alone sufficient to give him high rank among the writers of Spain.

> Blest night of wandering
> In secret, where by none might I be spied,
> Nor I see anything ;
> Without a light to guide,
> Save that which in my heart burnt in my side.
>
> That light did lead me on,
> More surely than the shining of noontide,
> Where well I knew that One
> Did for my coming bide ;
> Where he abode, might none but he abide.[1]

After his escape from prison, St. John wrote in quick succession his four chief works. *The Ascent of Mount Carmel* and *The Dark Night of the Soul* were completed before 1580. The first is an orderly treatise on the development of the spiritual life, intended for the use of those who have the care of souls. Its simple and yet lofty teaching, dealing chiefly with the purification of will, intellect, and senses, and utterly free from all insistence on the abnormal, shows how deeply Christian, how firmly based on ethics, was his conception of the relation of the soul to God. The whole book might indeed be regarded as a commentary on his own saying : " Man is created for God ; and is

[1] From the translation by Arthur Symons.

called to strip off all selfhood and unlikeness to Him." In *The Dark Night of the Soul* this stern demand for unlimited self-oblation and detachment —which had already been made, under other terms, by St. Ignatius—is applied even to the purest joys of the spiritual life, all of which the disciple is taught to sacrifice ; prizing the hours of aridity and interior darkness more than those of conscious communion, because these bring " diminished satisfaction with self."

Although St. John's teaching is always given in an objective and impersonal form, and is the work of a trained theologian depending on and familiar with the system of St. Thomas Aquinas; yet we feel here, far more than with many more exuberant mystics, that we are in close and detailed touch with personal experience of the highest kind. It was neither the confidences of St. Teresa, nor the ordinary teaching of the Church, which caused him to define contemplation as " nothing else but a secret, peaceful, and loving infusion of God " : the depth and essential sobriety of this conception reflect the condition which he had himself reached at the time when he wrote his chief works. He had then passed through and left behind alike the gloom and derelictions of the Dark Night, and those intense raptures and transient ecstasies, experienced in his imprisonment, which he calls the " spiritual betrothal " of the soul to God. Now, at over forty years of age, persecuted and ill, he had come to that steady and established certitude of essential, creative union, which alone he considers worthy to be called the " spiritual marriage " of the soul.

SPANISH MYSTICISM

What God communicates to the soul in this intimate union is utterly ineffable, beyond the reach of all possible words . . . in this state God and the soul are united as the window is with the light or the coal with the fire . . . this communication of God diffuses itself substantially in the whole soul, or rather the soul is transformed in God. In this transformation the soul drinks of God in its very substance and its spiritual powers.

The two books in which his purely mystical teachings are contained—*The Spiritual Canticle* and *The Flame of Living Love*—written between 1582 and 1584, are undoubtedly based upon memories of the ecstatic spiritual states through which he had passed in the course of his development. Their form is that of commentaries on the poems written during his imprisonment ; and they therefore represent the considered reflections of the mature contemplative on the graces and special experiences which had marked his growth. Only by considering together the hard and bracing doctrine of the earlier books, and these impassioned, indeed unequalled, descriptions of high mystical attainment, can we form a just idea of the character of St. John's mysticism ; the close connection that exists between its solid and sometimes unattractive foundations, and the lofty pinnacles with which it is crowned.

ILLUSTRATIVE WORKS

Graham, G. Cunninghame. St. Teresa : Her Life and Times. 2 vols. London, 1894.

Ignatius, St. The Spiritual Exercises. Spanish and English, with Commentary by J. Rickaby, S.J. London, 1915.
The Testament of. Translated by G. M. Rix. London, 1900.

THE MYSTICS OF THE CHURCH

John of the Cross, St.

The Ascent of Mount Carmel. Translated by D. Lewis. London, 1906.

The Dark Night of the Soul. Translated by D Lewis. London, 1916.

The Flame of Living Love. Translated by D. Lewis. London, 1912.

The Spiritual Canticle. Translated by D. Lewis. London, 1909.

Peers, Allison. Spanish Mysticism. London, 1924.

Teresa, St. Life. Written by Herself. Translated by D. Lewis. 5th edition. London, 1916.

The Book of the Foundations. Translated by D. Lewis. London, 1913.

The Way of Perfection. Translated by the Benedictines of Stanbrook. London, 1911.

The Interior Castle. Translated by the Benedictines of Stanbrook. London, 1912.

Letters, 4 vols. Translated by the Benedictines of Stanbrook. London, 1919–24.

Minor Works. Translated by the Benedictines of Stanbrook. London, 1913.

CHAPTER X

FRENCH SEVENTEENTH-CENTURY MYSTICISM

MADAME ACARIE—PIERRE DE BÉRULLE—ST. FRANÇOIS
DE SALES—ST. CHANTAL—MARIE DE L'INCARNA-
TION—PASCAL—BROTHER LAWRENCE—FÉNELON—
THE QUIETISTS

WE can hardly say of France, as of England and
Spain, that its chief contributions to mystical
history fall within a single century. Still, the
amazing period which opens with the career of
Madame Acarie (1566–1618) and fades away with
that of Madame Guyon (1648–1717) does form
a well-marked and peculiarly interesting epoch in
the spiritual history of the French Church. In
spite of the apparent worldliness and corruption
of the time, a network of spirituality, knotted and
sustained by great and saintly personalities, ran
through it ; and the vivid and intimate accounts
of these great personalities which have survived
enable us to get far nearer to them than we can
do in the case of the mediæval mystical saints.
France in the seventeenth century seems to have
been full of mystics of all types, from the simplest
to the most sophisticated. As in fourteenth-century
Italy and Germany, each gathered disciples ;
forming small groups devoted to an intensive

spiritual culture, in and through which the science of the inner life was studied and spread. These groups were closely related, and certain great souls and influences affected them all. Seldom indeed has the social aspect of the contemplative life been more richly developed.

Besides this, there are three other characters specially distinctive of this school. First, the fact that, historically speaking, French mysticism faded away into quietism represents the one-sided exaggeration of a trend present in it from the first ; that tendency to place the whole of religion in an unconditioned self-yielding to God, which easily glides into the cult of passivity. Yet this, after all, was a noble error : the shadowy side of that turning of the religious consciousness toward pure adoration and away from mere self-consideration, which is the glory of all the great French mystics. This " theocentric spirituality " is taught again and again by those spiritual directors of genius who were produced in such abundance at this time ; we may look upon it as one of the three essential characters of the school.

Secondly, French mysticism, if not the child, is at least the god-child of St. Teresa, and witnesses to the life-giving character of her career. The appearance in France of her writings, and the establishment in Paris of Carmelite nuns whom the saint had herself trained in the science of prayer, were decisive factors in its development. Directly or indirectly, all the great personalities of this epoch came into touch with Carmel and were salted by its salt ; and we cannot doubt that the active, concrete, very Christian character of Teresian mysticism was a powerful check on the quietistic tendencies of the French religious mind.

Thirdly, though sooner or later many of the great French mystics entered or formed religious communities, the leadership was frequently in lay hands. The " prophet " was recognized and valued as well as the " priest." Madame Acarie, M. de Bernières—the most widely-read of mystical writers —Madame Guyon, and many others instructed and directed souls, and it was thought right and natural that they should do so. No one found anything strange in such a career as that of the farm-servant Barbe of Compiègne, " for fifteen years directed solely by Christ," who formed and supported the inner life of the saintly and exquisite Antoinette de Jésus (born 1612), and became the acknowledged centre of a spiritual group visited by the celebrated Père Condren. Madame Guyon has been cruelly described as a " director of duchesses " ; and the immense influence exercised by the Carmelite lay-brother Lawrence, who began his life as a footman and spent much of it as the monastery cook, is well known.

From the crowded history of this immense mystical movement it is only possible to pick out a few significant names ; and looking into the facts, it becomes apparent that some of the most important are those which are now least known. The French religious renaissance owes its first mystical impulsion in a great degree to the influence of a forgotten Englishman. William Fitch (1520–1611)—known in religion as Benedict Canfield, from the Essex village in which he was born—was converted in middle age from a worldly life, and migrated to

France, where, at the age of sixty, he became a
Capuchin friar. A mystic of the Franciscan type,
ardent, speculative and poetic, he was during the
last twenty years of his life one of the chief spiritual
influences of the time. He taught the elements of
contemplative prayer to Pierre de Bérulle, the
founder of the Oratory, and to Madame Acarie.
He directed the inner life of the Benedictines of
Montmartre, whose convent became a forcing-
house of spirituality. His widely distributed book,
A Rule of Perfection, was used by two generations
of mystics. Thus he touched the religious life of
the century at all points, and in considering its
mystical side we are largely concerned with his
spiritual descendants.

This mystical side, complicated by the large
number of names of importance and the interaction
of its various groups, is best studied in three divi-
sions. First there are those mystics who flourished
in the first quarter of the century; all deeply
influenced by Madame Acarie, and often members
of her spiritual circle. Here the great and creative
personalities are Madame Acarie herself and her
Carmelite daughters ; Bérulle and his disciples
and associates, among whom we must place St.
Vincent de Paul (1581–1660) and Charles de
Condren (1588–1641) ; St. François de Sales
(1567–1622) and his pupil St. Chantal (1572–
1641.) Next, in the middle of the century, Pascal
(1623–62) and the school of Port Royal ; and
certain isolated mystics of the first rank, of whom
the most interesting are Marie de l'Incarnation
(1599–1672), who has been called " the Teresa
of France," and Brother Lawrence (1610–91).

Finally the period closes on the Quietist movement, now chiefly remembered in connection with Madame Guyon (1648–1717) and the unfortunate controversies which her teaching aroused. This time of declension is relieved by the great name of Fénelon (1651–1715), one of those inspired directors of souls who are characteristic of French religion at its best.

Madame Acarie, whose vigorous and saintly influence colours so strongly the first period of this astonishing epoch, refutes by the mere facts of her life those charges of incapacity and abstraction from practical life which are still brought against the mystics. Though she had as a child wished to become a nun, this desire was repressed ; and she married at sixteen a jovial and extravagant worldling, whose entangled affairs were a perpetual charge upon her care. She had six children.

Her mystical genius showed itself when she was twenty-two, and took at first a pronounced ecstatic form. But her long trances and other abnormal experiences, greatly as they impressed her friends and disciples, do not constitute Madame Acarie's chief claim upon our interest and reverence : they were merely the external signs of an absorption in God so intimate and complete that all her acts and words were controlled by invisible guidance, and made the instruments of an invisible Power. She always sought to hide these external signs from others. " Her deep and solid humility," said a contemporary witness, " was the veil which covered the *sancta sanctorum* of her soul."

According to those who knew her, she " hardly ever dealt with anyone, at least on matters of importance, unless with an inward vision wholly recollected and present before God ; and if this vision failed her she stopped short, seeming not to know where she was, and without caring what those with whom she dealt might think of it." Here was the source of that practical genius for the direction of souls, that irresistible spiritual contagion which was felt by all who came within her influence ; and which made of Madame Acarie, though she never wrote a line or sought to enlarge her sphere of action, one of the great creative personalities of her time.

Tormented by ill-health, walking on crutches, and forced to give much time to exacting domestic duties and the management of her husband's affairs, she yet became " the conscience of Paris " —a magnet towards whom for more than thirty years all who desired the life of the spirit inevitably found their way. She directed and stimulated a large group of disciples, and thousands of conversions were attributed to her. The exquisite and urbane François de Sales, coming as a young man to her house, there received his first definite impulsion towards that interior growth which made a delightful ecclesiastic into a man of mingled prayer and common sense, fit to guide and understand the soul of St. Chantal.

Constantly visiting the convents of Paris, where fervour and austerity of life were mostly at a low ebb, she everywhere roused a fresh ardour for God ; and her influence can be detected behind every incident of the spiritual revival in seventeenth-century France. Yet this great soul, who received from all that tribute of awe which only the saints can evoke, and whose countless good works were simply the continuance in action of her interior life with God, would always break off her ecstasies to join in her children's games, and never failed to be interested in every detail of the lives of those surrounding her.

When the life and works of St. Teresa were first translated into French, Madame Acarie—destined to introduce Teresian ideals into France and so give French mysticism a temper it has never lost— was not greatly impressed. This is perhaps easier to understand when we remember that much which is described in them was already a commonplace of her experience. But in two of those dream-like visions which influenced critical periods of her life she believed that St. Teresa appeared in person and announced that it was God's will that she should bring the reformed Carmelites to Paris. Encouraged by François de Sales, Bérulle, and other members of her circle, Madame Acarie therefore launched a movement for the establishment of a Carmelite convent. She also took into her house, and trained for several years, a group of postulants, who afterwards became the first French Carmelite nuns. Chosen and formed by this truly Teresian mystic, who yet continued to live as a married woman in the world, none of St. Teresa's own novices exhibited in greater perfection that union of sanctity with practicality on which she laid such stress.

After endless difficulties six Spanish nuns, of whom two had been the companions of the saint, were brought to France in order that perfect continuity with the actual method and spirit of Teresa might be assured ; thus exhibiting again that historical character which has always marked the genuine mysticism of the Christian Church. The first house was opened in Paris in 1604 ; and when Madame Acarie died, fourteen years later, France possessed seventeen convents of reformed Carmelites, where the mystical life was lived in its purity and its secrets were disseminated, not only among the novices, but to all who came to the parlours and talked to the experts behind the grille.

The establishment of these convents meant far more than a mere multiplication of religious houses for women. It meant the appearance within the French Church of real homes where the life of the spirit could be cultivated, and whence its light could spread : the life-giving life of St. Teresa bearing fruit in a new sphere. The coming of the Carmelites, so closely connected with the sanctified wisdom and indomitable will of Madame Acarie, was the next phase in that spiritual revival which had its first home in her *salon*, and its first expression in her immense personal influence on souls. The last four years of her life, after her husband's death, were spent in the humble position of a lay-sister under the authority of one of her own daughters ; an end witnessing more surely to her greatness of soul than the ecstasies and activities for which she is generally known.

All Madame Acarie's three daughters became Carmelite nuns. The youngest, Marguerite, was perhaps, of all the mystics of this period, the one who best translated the spirit of St. Teresa into French terms. Gay, frank, vivacious, those who knew her declared that her simple manner and breezy speech, her hatred of religious ostentation and intensity, concealed a contemplative experience and supernatural intuition even exceeding that of her mother. Her remark to a nun who had tried to assume an appropriately severe appearance—" There is no sin in being thought silly, but there may easily be sin in trying to look so correct. Do let yourself be natural ! " would have delighted St. Teresa ; and proves better than any ecstasy, any ferocious austerities, that the spirit of the Foundress was re-born in the Carmelites of France. " The interior life," said Mother Marguerite, " consists in very few words, and a very great tendency to God."

It was from the French Carmelites of Dijon that St. Chantal received her first mystical education. Thus her Order of the Visitation, a capital creation of French mysticism, traces one line of its descent from St. Teresa, and the other from the pure Gallican school as represented in Pierre de Bérulle (1575–1629) and in its co-founder, St. François de Sales. Bérulle, the creator of the Oratory and for long the director of Madame Acarie, wrote little ; but was, through his work as a religious founder, and as trainer of countless individual souls, one of the most influential personalities of the century, touching every great mystic of the time. He best represents the doctrinal side of French mysticism, saturating and transforming dogmatic theology with his own intense consciousness of God.

It was largely due to Bérulle that this movement became and remained so profoundly theocentric in character. Where many teachers of the contemplative life begin with the human soul, its purification, growth and enlightenment, Bérulle always begins with God. For him, adoration is the primary spiritual act ; and the state of perfect adherence to God, is all that is really asked of men. This pure and lofty teaching, free from all taint of religious self-interest, produced beautiful and saintly characters wherever Bérulle's influence reached ; and continued, long after his death, to give its colour to French theology. To him, in a great degree, we owe the formation of the exquisite yet ever active St. Vincent de Paul (1581–1660); that pattern of practical mystics, of whom it has been well said that he was charitable because he was a saint, not a saint because he was charitable. For St. Vincent de Paul, intimate with St. François de Sales and St. Chantal, Bérulle— who has received no aureole from the Church— was yet " one of the holiest men I have known . . . of a *solid* sanctity which you will hardly find elsewhere ! " Such words make us realize the frank and intimate relations existing between these great French mystics, whose diverse natures and vocations all served one end.

So close, indeed, were these relations, that in studying one we are obliged to study all. Thus the spiritual experience of Jeanne-François de Chantal (1572–1641), Foundress of the Visitation, emerges from that of the French Carmelites and is affected by Bérulle ; whilst her long and intimate connection with St. François de Sales— himself, perhaps, hardly to be called a mystic, though incomparable as a controller and educator of mystical souls—provides one of the most interesting and subtle of studies in spiritual relationships.

The elements which contributed to the making of this mystic, and so of her Order, witness in a remarkable manner to the interaction of human spirits working towards a hidden goal.

Madame de Chantal was a well-born and attractive woman, warmly affectionate and naturally pious, in whom a pronounced mystical genius was balanced by a touching dependence on those human friendships which adorned the whole of her life. Married at twenty to a man whom she adored, and widowed at twenty-eight, her ardent temperament poured itself into the religious channel. After a period of much spiritual suffering and unrest she came first under the influence of St. François de Sales, which remained for nearly twenty years the governing fact of her personal life ; and then, when she was thirty-four, under that of the Carmelites of Dijon, at this time ruled by the austere and holy Anne of Jesus, the companion of St. Teresa.

This double guidance was perfectly adapted to her needs. Whilst the Carmelites trained her emerging contemplative faculty, and explained to her the adventures of her soul, the prudence and psychological skill of St. François, his gentle yet steady insistence on complete self-conquest as the one thing needful, gave her that background of sane asceticism which the mystical life always requires. The Carmelites showed her the way up the mountains : he trained her spiritual muscles for the ascent. To the end he continued the firm schooling of her soul and character. " What does it matter whether God speaks to us from among thorns or flowers ? " he says in 1607, when she has been three years under his direction ; and, twelve years later, when the " very dear daughter " has become the Rev. Mother Superior of the Visitation, this most gentle of directors, who requires " all to be done by love and nothing by force," continues on the same bracing note to urge on her those last renunciations so difficult to her very human heart. " Do not think any more either of the friendship or the unity God has made between us, nor of your children, your heart, nor your soul—in fact, of anything whatever, for you have given *all* to God." In return for this faithful discipline and support, St. Chantal opened up to her director reaches of spirituality he could not have achieved alone, and made the author of *An Introduction to the Devout Life* capable of writing the *Treatise of the Love of God*.

Their long and intimate friendship, one of the most beautiful in religious history, brought into existence the Order of the Visitation—so perfectly representative of the ideals of both. In this Order, intended to provide a home for those who were drawn to the spiritual life of the Carmelites, but were not capable of their physical austerities, the gentle moderation and insistence on essentials, which characterized the teaching of St. François, leavens the mystical ardour of St. Chantal. " I desire," said St. François, " to give daughters of contemplation to God." " Our Institute," said St. Chantal, " is *wholly based* on the inner life "— but in such a manner that " no great harshness should turn the weak and infirm from joining it, there to devote themselves to the perfection of Divine Love."

This separation of the spiritual life from the externals of asceticism was thought almost comic by the pious persons of the time, who accused the founders of setting up "a nursing-home rather than a religious house." It marked, as a matter of fact, a genuine forward movement in the corporate expression of Christian mysticism ; and the originality and importance of St. François and St. Chantal consists in the fact that they realized and gave form to this ideal. At first the Visitandines divided their time between contemplation and active works of charity, visiting the sick and poor ; but they gradually found themselves drawn more and more to a life of complete retirement and prayer, and in 1615 became definitely enclosed. Our opinion of this change will depend on the social worth which we attribute to an existence wholly concentrated on God.

The work of St. François on *The Love of God*, representing by declaration the fruits of his communion with the first Visitation nuns, is a vivid picture of the secret life of the Community. Under his wise direction, that which might easily have been a hot-bed of feverish religiosity became a true home of contemplative prayer.

Our blessed Father (said one of the early Visitandines) wished that, to increase humility, our Sisters should take turns with the cooking and domestic work. Our blessed Mother (St. Chantal) never excused herself, save for illness, from being cook in her turn. . . . It is true, that which he chiefly cared for and loved best was to ground his daughters well in the true inward life of the Spirit, to which all were much drawn ; so that they sought nothing for themselves but mortification, recollection, silence, and hiddenness in God.

And the result of this balanced training, this

life of mingled homeliness and loftiness, is shown to us by St. Chantal herself, when she declares, in a phrase that sums up the essential attitude of the mystic :

The almost universal tendency of the daughters of the Visitation is to a very simple practice of the Presence of God, by an entire self-abandonment to His holy Providence.

These words inevitably bring to mind one of the best known and loved of the French mystics— Brother Lawrence, of the *Practice of the Presence of God*—who was born in the year in which the Visitation was founded. His little book is sometimes described as " simple," but its simplicity is that of the heights. Brother Lawrence reveals hardly anything of the stages and disciplines which are so prominent in the lives of most mystics. He tells us of the sudden conversion when he was eighteen, which detached him once for all from the world and self-interest, and filled him with the love of God ; how he was by profession a footman, " a great awkward fellow, who broke everything," and, becoming a Carmelite lay-brother, expected to suffer much for his faults ; how for four years he endured great trouble of mind, and thence passed to a " perfect liberty and continual joy," which upheld him equally during his work in the monastery kitchen (which he naturally disliked) and during set times of prayer. So much indeed were action and contemplation interfused, that he ceased to perceive much difference between them.

Such freedom and suppleness of soul—a characteristic on which François de Sales and Lawrence lay equal stress—means in practice a level of spirituality which is less startling, but far more complete, than the entranced contemplations of the ecstatic withdrawn from active affairs. St. Teresa leaving her enclosure to found houses of religion all over Spain, Madame Acarie emerging from rapture to join the children's games, Lawrence " without any turn for business " going into Burgundy to buy wine for his convent " without uneasiness, saying to God it was His business he was about . . . and afterwards finding it very well performed," witness in their various ways to a real transfiguration of human personality, completely transfused by the Divine power and love.

The letters of Brother Lawrence, mostly written in old age to those who asked his advice—for like all the mystics of this rich period, so hungry for the spiritual life, his quality was recognized and he attracted many disciples—testify to the fullness with which this life had been established in him.

He is now (he says of himself) so accustomed to that *Divine Presence* that he receives from it continual succour upon all occasions. For above thirty years, his soul has been filled with joys so continual and sometimes so transcendent, that he is forced to use means to moderate them and to prevent their appearing outwardly.

If sometimes he is a little too much absent from that *Divine Presence*, which happens often when he is most engaged in his outward business, God presently makes Himself felt in his soul to recall him. He answers with exact fidelity to these inward drawings, either by an elevation of his heart towards God, or by a meek and loving regard to Him, or by such words as love forms upon these occasions, as, for instance, *My God, behold me, wholly Thine* ; *Lord, make me according to Thy heart.* And then it seems to him (as in effect he feels it) that this God of love, satisfied with such few words, reposes again and rests in the depth and centre of his soul. The experience of these things gives him such an assurance that God is always deep within his soul, that no doubt of it can arise, whatever may betide.

Another mystic, hardly known to modern readers, yet with far greater powers of expression, exhibits perhaps even more clearly this gradual remaking and final emancipation of the self. Marie Guyard, or Martin, afterwards known as Marie de l'Incarnation (1599–1672), was born at Tours, of the commercial class. She was married at eighteen, and at twenty-one was left a widow with one child. It was at this time that her first great mystical experience took place : an overwhelming sight of her own sin and imperfection, which filled her with remorse and love. She now lived for ten years a busy practical life, helping in the family business, yet always, like Lawrence, " in the presence of God "—or, as she expresses it with her customary struggle for exactitude, in a state of " tendency " to Him. This represents the first stage of her mystical growth. It was succeeded by a period of intense emotional rapture, from about her twenty-seventh to thirtieth year ; marked by two great ecstatic experiences, by violent alternations between contemplation and desolation, and by a lyrical joy which often found outward expression, reminding us of Richard Rolle's " state of song."

It was towards the end of this spiritual adolescence that Madame Martin yielded to her longing for a definitely religious life, and became an Ursuline nun ; going nine years later at the head of a small band of Sisters to Canada as an educational and religious pioneer—a heroic adventure for a woman of her time. There, beset by constant anxieties and exacting work, the rest of her life was spent ; and there she achieved that supple maturity of soul which has earned for her the name of " the Teresa of France." As with her great prototype, her ecstatic experiences practically ceased when this, the constructive period of her life, began. She developed instead a steady and quiet state of union with God, which persisted through the innumerable and apparently distracting activities that filled her days.

Her descriptions of this interior evolution deserve to rank with those of the greatest contemplative saints :

My spirit (she says) became more and more simplified, making fewer and fewer inward or outward acts which could cause feeling. But my soul in its depths said continually these words : " Oh my Love, be Thou blessed " ; or even these alone, " My God, my God ! " These fundamental words filled me with sweet food, but without any feeling. Our Lord also took from me the great transports and violent seizures, and since then my soul has dwelt in her centre, which is God, and this centre is in herself where she is above all feeling. This is so simple and delicate a thing that she cannot express it. One can read, write, work, do what one will, and nevertheless this fundamental occupation always abides, and the soul never ceases to be united to God. Even the immensities of God in no way divert her ; but without stopping at them, she remains attached to God in her simplicity." . . .

When I go about the house or when I walk in the garden, I feel my heart constrained by continual impulses of love ; and sometimes it seems that this heart must rush forth and as it were leave its own place. But although the inferior part suffers much, the superior part feels more vigorous, and more able to act with greater purity and delicacy ; because she is not involved with anything that hinders her, and sends nothing to the senses but keeps all in her own depths. . . .

This third state of prayer is the most sublime . . . the senses are in it so free, that the soul which has attained it can act in it without distraction in all the employments her condition requires. It is a permanent, or better a continuous state, wherein the soul remains calm in such wise that nothing can distract her. . . .

If business, either necessary or indifferent, brings certain objects before the imagination, these are only little clouds, like those which pass before the sun and only take away the sight of it for an instant. And even during this moment God shines in the deeps of the soul, which is as it were waiting, like a person who is interrupted when she speaks to another and who nevertheless still looks at him to whom she spoke. She is as it were waiting in silence, and presently returns to her intimate union.

These quotations, chiefly from letters to her son and biographer, Dom Claude, are given at length because they mark so well the broadening and deepening of spiritual outlook, the increased, tranquil understanding of the relation in which contemplation should stand to the whole complex of Christian life, which the Church owes to the great mystics of this time. They take up the science of prayer where the mediæval saints left it, and bring out its richest implications. They are " psychologists " in the true sense of that ill-used word. Marie de l'Incarnation *lives* that two-fold life of " adoration and adherence " in which Bérulle had declared the whole duty and joy of a spiritual man to consist ; her life and his doctrine sum up the gift of this school of mystics to the Church. In their English Catholic contemporaries, the Benedictine contemplative Augustine Baker (1575–1641) and his pupil Dame Gertrude More (1606–33), we again find this balanced outlook ; and through the writings of these mystics, whose religious life was chiefly lived on French soil, the genius of French mysticism touched and affected later generations of English contemplatives. The teachings of Augustine Baker, collected in the book called *Holy Wisdom*, still provide one of the best of all pilot books for unskilled voyagers on that which Ruysbroeck called " the vast and stormy

Sea of the Divine." Mediæval fervour and Bene-dictine wisdom are here blended, and infused by that talent for the "discerning of spirits" and directing of souls which was a special character of French spirituality.

The mysticism of the mid-seventeenth century represents a development of the doctrine taught on the one hand by the first Oratorians, especially Bérulle and his great disciple Charles de Condren (1588–1641) and by Olier (1608–57) of St. Sulpice ; on the other by St. François de Sales. Its best known expression is found among the contemplative souls who were attached to the famous Abbey of Port Royal. The story of this hot-bed of personal religion is too well known to need repetition here. Its puritanical rigorisms were sweetened by a real mystical passion, which took its colour from the great French masters of the contemplative life ; again demonstrating the close social solidarity which united in this period even the most diverse of the seekers for reality. The Jansenism of Port Royal was, largely, an unbalanced exaggeration of that vivid sense of the soul's respon-sibility and realness, which is natural to the mystic ; and St.-Cyran, its most celebrated and unfortunate representative, seems in his secret life to have been an uneasy contemplative, who sought without much success to model himself on St. François de Sales.

The really mystical side of Port Royal is seen in two sharply contrasted personalities. The beauti-ful spirit of Mère Agnes (1593–1671) fed by the teachings of Bérulle and his followers, continues the best traditions of French spirituality, its lofty theocentricism, its tendency to abstract contemplation. At the opposite extreme, Pascal (1623–62) escapes from the attacks of his self-tormenting nature and his intellectual unrest by way first of the ecstatic experience recorded in the celebrated *Amulet* ; then of the impassioned Christocentric devotion which finds expression in the exquisite *Mystère de Jésus*. These are the two great moments of his mystical life. In the *Amulet* or *Memorial* —that scrap of parchment, so fortunately preserved for us, which he wore on his person from 1654 until his death—we have the stammering phrases in which he had tried to recapture the " Certitude and Joy " of an overwhelming revelation of God : a revelation satisfying in full his thirst for that living Reality, that " Universal Being " which, as he says in the *Pensées*, " it is the nature of the heart to love."

From about half-past ten in the evening (says the *Memorial*) till about half an hour after midnight : Fire ! God of Abraham. God of Isaac. God of Jacob. Not of philosophers and scholars . . . the world has not known Thee, but I have known Thee. Joy, joy, joy ; tears of joy !

In the meditation called the *Mystère de Jésus* intimacy and love complete the work of adoration. The very heart of Christocentric mysticism is here unveiled to us by means of a few curt sentences, of which the holy magic owes nothing to literary art. " We know many things more sublime," says Brémond of this tiny masterpiece, " but nothing more contagious." In virtue of this gift and its influence Pascal—who might from one point of view be regarded as a lonely intellectualist—wins a place among the creative mystics of the Church.

The end of the seventeenth century saw the

gradual fading away of this great mystical epoch :
and, as in most periods of decadence, it was in the
unbalanced exaggeration of certain essential characters, the suppression of others, that its progressive
disintegration was shown. Quietism, the characteristic religious movement of this time, represents
the excessive stressing of that passive element
which had always been present in French mysticism,
its abstraction from the complex of tendencies which
together make up a healthy spiritual life. Now
best known in the work of Madame Guyon (1648–
1717), that busy lady is, as a matter of fact, far
from being the typical Quietist. This parody of the
contemplative life had appeared early in the century
in the wrong-headed fervour of Antoinette Bourig-
nan (1616–80) and was continued by her disciple,
Peter Poiret (1646–1719), and by Malaval, the
blind cleric of Marseilles. Behind Madame Guyon
is the tragic figure of the Spanish priest Molinos
(1640–97), executed for the real or supposed
moral errors which his doctrine of passivity was
believed to involve.

In spite of its manifest exaggerations, Quietism
has considerable historical importance. It influenced, though not always to their advantage, such
differing religious temperaments as those of the
early Quakers and William Blake. In it the rich
spiritual movement which had formed Bérulle,
François de Sales, and their contemporaries became
thin, precious, self-conscious. Its most celebrated
exponent, the unfortunate Madame Guyon, provides one of the most instructive caricatures of true
sanctity to be found in the whole history of the
Church—a caricature which is all the more effective

because it approaches so closely to its model at many points. But for her persistent self-occupation and her lack of common sense, Madame Guyon might actually have become the mystical saint she supposed herself to be ; and since her best known book, *A Short and Easy Method of Prayer*, is still much read and admired, and its author commonly classed among the great Christian mystics, it seems worth while to draw attention to some features in her career and doctrine which are commonly overlooked.

Madame Guyon was a well-born and very beautiful woman, full of charm, who grew up in the period following that of the great French mystics ; a moment in which they were widely read and admired, and the fatal inclination to copy the contemplative life in cheaper materials had already appeared. Her natural religious enthusiasm had therefore plenty on which to feed. An unhappy marriage increased her inclination to piety. She practised ferocious mortifications ; and, having learnt from a monk to whom she went for direction that simple " prayer of interior silence " which has been so greatly used by the saints, she promptly elevated it into the whole substance of the mystical life. The result was a cult of passivity and self-abandonment, so excessive that it was inevitably condemned by all religious teachers in touch with the realities of the human soul. At the height of her development Madame Guyon insisted on a " holy indifference " which left no room for any exercise of the will, which did not admit of contrition, and did not even prefer heaven rather than hell. This level of absurdity, however, was only

gradually achieved, and represents the uncriticized exaggeration of a doctrine which was in its
beginnings of a harmlessly traditional sort.

Left a widow at twenty-eight, the career of
St. Chantal suggested to her what her own future
might be ; and unfortunately she found in the
Barnabite Père La Combe, the person who seemed
destined to play in it the part of a second St.
François de Sales. The new saints, however, felt
an intense interest in themselves and each other,
which their models would hardly have approved.
It was not long before Madame Guyon, who was
greatly venerated by the pious aristocracy, came to
believe that she was the new corner-stone of the
Church and the Woman clothed with the Sun
of the Apocalypse ; whilst her interior union
with Père La Combe became so perfect that she
declared herself unable to distinguish him from
God. There is no need to continue the elabora-
tion of this story ; but its main features must be
remembered when we try to estimate the value
of Madame Guyon's spiritual works. These run
to forty volumes, of several hundred pages each ;
and some at least were written, by her own account,
in an " inspired " or automatic state. The *Method
of Prayer* which is alone familiar to modern readers,
is at once the shortest and most sane.

It was not until 1688, when she was nearly
forty and at the height of her religious reputation,
that Madame Guyon came into contact with
Fénelon, with whose soul, unfortunately, she
" found that hers was in perfect harmony." It is
one of the puzzles of religious history that this
well-meaning, but certainly self-deluded, preacher

of mysticality managed to persuade the exquisite scholar and skilled director of souls that she was indeed a prophetess and a saint. Possibly the absence on both sides of a strong sense of humour contributed to this disastrous situation and its results. Though the Quietism defended by Fénelon in his celebrated *Maxims*, and afterwards condemned by authority, is a very innocent form of passivity—going indeed little beyond that principle of loving and unlimited surrender to God which has been practised and taught by the greatest mystical saints—the notoriety of Madame Guyon's more extreme utterances, her ever-increasing volubility, and, above all, the painful atmosphere of controversy which now surrounded all these questions, prevented its true bearing from being understood. More gentle methods proving useless, Madame Guyon and Père La Combe were imprisoned. Fénelon, whose generous advocacy had been both misunderstood and exploited, was broken and disgraced.

Yet this, the apparent death-agony of a great mystical epoch, had in it the seeds of life. From the retirement in which his last sixteen years were spent, Fénelon, spiritualized by adversity, wrote the greater number of those " letters of direction," full of wise and skilled advice on the life of love and prayer, by which he still continues his influence on souls. Through these the noble spirit of French mysticism was preserved and bore fruit, in times and places where its major products were unknown. Thus Fénelon reached and affected the eighteenth-century Quakers, the leaders of the Evangelical revival, the Tractarians ; and, in his own country, taught, and still teaches, those who continue the great Gallican tradition of the spiritual life.

ILLUSTRATIVE WORKS

Brémond, H.   Histoire Littéraire du Sentiment Religieux en France.   6 vols.   Paris, 1923.

St. Chantal.   Paris, 1912.

Chantal, St. Jane Frances de.   Her Spirit as shown in her Letters.   London, 1922.

Fénelon.   Spiritual Letters to Men.   Translated by Sidney Lear.   London, 1880.

Spiritual Letters to Women.   Translated by Sidney Lear.   London, 1906.

Spiritual Letters to Ecclesiastics, Religious, etc. London, 1892.

François de Sales, St.   Introduction to the Devout Life. Translated by Rev. A. Ross.   London, 1925.

Treatise of the Love of God.   Edited by W. J. Knox Little.   London, 1901.

Spiritual Letters.   Translated by Sidney Lear. London, 1892.

Guyon, Madame.   A Short and Easy Method of Prayer. London, 1900.

Autobiography.   Translated by T. Allen, 2 vols. London, 1897.

Huvelin, Abbé.   Quelques Directeurs d'Ames au XVII Siècle.   3rd edition.   Paris, 1923.

Lawrence, Brother.   The Practice of the Presence of God. London, 1906.

Pascal.   Pensées, Fragments, et Lettres.   Paris, 1897.

Sanders, E. K.   Fénelon, his Friends and Enemies. London, 1901.

Angélique of Port Royal.   London, 1905.

Vincent de Paul.   London, 1913.

St. Chantal.   London, 1918.

CHAPTER XI

SOME PROTESTANT MYSTICS

BOEHME—ANGELUS SILESIUS—THE MYSTICAL POETS
AND CAMBRIDGE PLATONISTS—FOX AND THE
QUAKERS—WILLIAM LAW—HENRY MARTYN

It will seem to many readers that an excessive space has so far been given to Mysticism in the Catholic Church, especially since the emphasis placed by the Protestant reformers on personal rather than institutional religion might be expected to encourage the mystical approach to God and produce a flourishing school of mystics. It is one of the curiosities of religious history that this does not seem to have been the case. Luther, it is true, had his mystical side. The Lutheran " faith," which is the foundation-stone of his theology, has far more the character of mystical adherence to God than of mere belief. He was deeply influenced by the *Theologia Germanica*, and in his popular preaching continued many of the ideas of the German mystics. But this aspect of his reform died with him, and mysticism has never been really at home in the Lutheran—still less in the Calvinistic—branch of the Church.

The great achievements of the mediæval mystics had been accomplished within a home atmosphere which, if it sometimes cramped them, certainly gave them nourishment, discipline, support; and left their spiritual energies free to respond fully to God. The Protestant mystics of the post-Reformation were, on the contrary, inhabitants of a house in which building operations were still going on. The sound of the hammer seems often to break in upon their quietude, and the anxious search for a suitable environment gives them an air of unrest. In their periods of self-conquest they are necessarily individualists, and have no ascetic scheme on which to rely. Hence the spiritual miseries of Bunyan, or the " perpetual hurly-burly, pulling and hauling, warring, fighting, struggling and striving " which Jacob Boehme endured and described. Clearly, lack of supporting tradition and religious unrest increased these sufferings, and acted prejudicially on many of these true prophets and saints. Finding no food in external religion, they became hostile to it, and set up a false opposition between personal experience of God and " outward forms." Some tended to Quietism ; others wandered off into realms of speculation, invented strange doctrines, and mistook their personal experiences for the authoritative revelation of objective truths. In consequence, many were bitterly persecuted by the official Protestant Churches, which showed themselves, in the true spirit of the *parvenu*, more intolerant than Rome itself towards claims to individual enlightenment.

The post-Reformation was a great time for " religious views," most of which are now forgotten. But some of these views sprang from and witnessed to a genuine mystical experience, and continued their influence long after their author's death. The outstanding example of this is Jacob Boehme (1575–1624), one of the most original and astonishing of the Christian mystics. Of peasant origin, he was born near Görlitz, on the borders of Saxony and Silesia, and spent the greater part of his life as a cobbler. He was of an abnormal psychic constitution : a brooding visionary, easily passing into automatic states. Of such material the religious passion can make a great prophet ; and Boehme had the religious passion from the first. Even as a boy he craved for the reality of God. His spiritual history, much of which can be recovered from the personal references in his works, shows the phases through which a mystical genius passes, wholly uninfluenced by the traditional Catholic scheme. During adolescence he suffered much from the inward conflicts, torturing doubts, and unruly desires, with which all students of the mystics are familiar : " I went through a long and sore conflict before I obtained my noble garland." This stage ended in a mystical experience wherein he seemed for seven days of intense happiness " enwrapt in the Divine Light." This event, which he regarded as his true consecration, took place when he was about nineteen. But the joy and peace which he then experienced failed to silence his intellectual questionings, perpetually revolving round the problem of evil.

I fell into a very deep melancholy and heavy sadness, when I beheld and contemplated the great deep of this world, and considered in my spirit the whole creation of this world. Wherein then I found to be in all things evil and good, love and anger, in the inanimate creatures, viz. in wood, stones, earth and the elements, as also in men and beasts. . . .

But when in this affliction and trouble I elevated my spirit (for

I then understood very little or not at all what it was) I earnestly raised it up into God, as with a great storm or onset; wrapping up my whole heart and mind, as also all my thoughts and whole will and resolution, incessantly to wrestle with the love and mercy of God, and not to give over until He blessed me, that is until He enlightened me with His holy spirit, whereby I might understand His will, and be rid of my sadness. And then the spirit did break through.

This reference is clearly to the great ecstatic vision of the year 1600, when gazing one day at a bright pewter dish which reflected the sunlight, he suddenly fell into a trance. Then the long-sought gate was opened, and he attained once for all the incommunicable mystic certitude. In one quarter of an hour

I saw and knew more than if I had been many years at a University . . . the Being of Beings, the Byss and Abyss . . . the essential nature of evil and of good . . . The greatness of the triumphing that was in the spirit I cannot express . . . in this Light my spirit suddenly saw through all, and in and by all the creatures, even in herbs and grass, it knew God—who He is and how He is and what His will is—and suddenly in that Light my will was set on by a mighty impulse to describe the Being of God.

In this characteristic description, written twelve years after the event, we see how large a speculative and philosophic element entered into Boehme's mysticism. His spiritual demands ranged from that sense of personal communion which has satisfied many of the saints, to a world-view which should justify the ways of God. Even more thoroughly than Meister Eckhart, he doubles the parts of the philosopher and contemplative. In the next paragraph of the *Aurora*, the meditative cast of his mind becomes apparent. As Julian of Norwich pondered for years the meaning of her

" revelation of love," so Boehme quickly realized that he " could not at once apprehend " and " there passed almost twelve years before the exact understanding thereof was given me." In other words, the formless but convincing cosmic revelation was gradually reduced by him to conceptual images.

There is not much doubt that this " exact understanding " was helped by the reading of those alchemic and hermetic books then so much in vogue, from which he obtained the greater part of his vocabulary. The result is that in dealing with his voluminous and very difficult writings, we are called upon to distinguish the element of genuine revelation from the unconscious memories of suggestive phrases and ideas obtained from the common stock of German theosophy. This task may often seem hopeless, and indeed it is doubtful whether it will ever be completely performed. Yet the personal confessions scattered through his books constantly reveal the depth and simplicity of his soul ; its child-like dependence on that " Heart of God " in which " he sought to hide himself." It is in his combination of this deep quiet sense of personal communion with God, and an utter certitude that he had indeed been given a revelation of His creative method, a " ground-plan of the universe," that Boehme is unique among the mystics. The two aspects of experience interlock—only the pure in heart perceive the invisible realities of the " great Deep."

Where will you seek for God ? Seek Him in your soul that is proceeded out of the eternal nature, the living fountain of forces wherein the Divine working stands.

SOME PROTESTANT MYSTICS

O that I had but the pen of a man, and were able therewith to write down the spirit of knowledge! I can but stammer of great mysteries like a child that is beginning to speak; so very little can the earthly tongue express of that which the spirit comprehends.

It was at the close of these twelve years of brooding upon his great revelation—a period, we might say, of spiritual and also mental education—that a "vehement impulse" urged him to write down what he knew. The result was his first book, *The Aurora*, largely, according to his own account (which internal evidence confirms), the result of automatic composition:

Art has not written here, neither was there any time to consider how to set it down punctually, according to the understanding of the letters, but all was ordered according to the direction of the Spirit, which often went in haste, so that in many words letters may be wanting, and in some places a capital letter for a word; so that *the Penman's hand*, by reason that he was not accustomed to it, did often shake. And though I could have wrote in a more accurate, fair, and plain manner, yet the reason was this, that the burning fire often forced forward with speed, and the hand and pen must hasten directly after it; for it goes and comes like a sudden shower.

This strange mixture of "Philosophie, Astrologie and Theologie . . . set down diligently from a true ground in the knowledge of the Spirit and the impulse of God" introduces us to Boehme's intensely dualistic yet essentially Platonic conception of reality; governed by the two hostile principles of "the eternal darkness and the eternal light," which "couch within" the visible world and the living soul. It is hardly surprising that *The Aurora* offended local orthodoxy; and its author was forbidden to write again. For six years he remained silent; but the circulation of the work in MS. had brought him many learned and distinguished, and probably some eccentric, friends and admirers, under pressure from whom he again began to write in 1618 ; an unfortunate enrichment of his alchemic and astrological vocabulary keeping pace with his mystical development. Between this date and 1624 he produced an immense mass of writings, each in his own opinion " ten times deeper " than the last ; for his spiritual vision matured, and with each fresh " flash " he perceived how crude and approximate the earlier revelations had been.

It was in 1620 that Boehme declared himself to have reached the " lovely bright day " of full and peaceful illumination ; and his most lucid and spiritual works—the *Six Theosophic Points*, *Supersensual Dialogues*, and lovely *Way to Christ* with its truly mystical emphasis on religious realism and the personal responsibility of the soul—were all written after this date. In these books his thought sometimes finds a wonderfully simple and direct expression ; and has opened up for many a path along which it seems possible to reconcile the ruthless energy of nature with the peace and gentleness of God " wherein all worketh and willeth in quiet love."

For of God and in Him are all things ; darkness and light, love and anger, fire and light ; but He calleth Himself God only as to the light of His love. . . . Our whole teaching is nothing else than how a man should kindle in himself God's light-world. We live and are in God ; we have heaven and hell in ourselves. What we make of ourselves that we are : if we make of ourselves an angel, and dwell in the light and love of God in Christ, we are so ; but if we make of ourselves a fierce, false and haughty devil which contemns all love and meekness in mere covetousness, greedy hunger and thirst, then also we are so.

Ultimately his doctrine, in so far as it is amenable to analysis, is a doctrine of " will and desire." Man is regenerated and " saved " by effort as well as grace. He must strive for the " noble garland " ; first by self-conquest, and then by an energetic and progressive self-yielding to the Will of God, " harnessing his fiery energies to the service of the light." To elude this obligation is to be at best a " mere historical new man," and miss beatitude : for " heaven and hell are present everywhere, and it is but the turning of the *will* either into God's love or into His wrath, that introduceth into them."

The right of Boehme, with his complete independence of institutional religion, his outspoken criticism of " churches of stone " and their services and sacraments, to a place among the mystics of the Church, rests upon the great contribution which he undoubtedly made to the development of Christian experience. He was creative. His influence, during the century following his death, was felt strongly ; and nowhere more than in England, where certain aspects of the Quaker movement, and afterwards the mystical revival associated with William Law, are largely the results of his teaching.

A Christian (he said) is of no sect : he can dwell in the midst of sects and appear in their services, without being attached or bound to any.

And this seems to have been the destiny of his doctrine. Though at first sight he may seem a " lonely prophet," this appearance of isolation is illusory. He does not, for all his intuitive experience—and few mystics give so vivid an impression of first-hand communion with the unseen—escape the influence of tradition. Two lines of spiritual descent unite in him. On the one hand, he is a channel through which the teaching of the early German mystics—Eckhart, Tauler, the " German Theology "—affected the Protestant world. This teaching probably came to him at second-hand through the books of Valentine Weigel (1533–88) and his school, whose influence upon him can be established. On the other hand, through the current hermetic and theosophic literature which made so obvious an appeal to his mind, Boehme descends from Paracelsus, and the "nature-philosophers " of the Renaissance : and it was by means of imagery drawn from these sources that he struggled to give his vision concrete form. At his death in 1624 he was already deeply reverenced, not only by contemporary theologians, but also by philosophers and men of science. His influence was not limited to the reformed Churches, but by a curious turn of fortune it found its way even into the Catholic fold. Among those who owed their first enlightenment to his writings was Johann Scheffler (1624–77) commonly known as Angelus Silesius ; the son of a Polish nobleman, and Court physician to the Emperor Frederic III. Scheffler's *Divine Epigrams* sufficiently attest the degree in which Boehme had influenced his thought ; even without the well-known lines which he dedicated to him :

> In Water lives the fish, the plant in Earth abides,
> The bird in Air, the sun in Firmament.
> In burning Fire the salamander hides,
> God's Heart is Jacob Boehme's element !

Nevertheless, the ardently personal character of Scheffler's mysticism finally reached a point at which it could not be satisfied by Boehme's doctrines. He abjured them, entered the Roman Catholic Church in 1661, and became a Franciscan friar. In the poems which he wrote during this final period of his life—among them the famous hymn

> O Love, who formedst me to wear
> The image of Thy Godhead here!

—he appears as the spiritual heir of Jacopone da Todi and the great Franciscan mystics ; who are thus brought by converging streams of spiritual influence into unexpected contact with the " Teutonic philosopher " of Görlitz.

The translation of Boehme's works into English began in 1644, and was completed in 1661. As the lifeless and worldly character of the official Church had provoked in Germany a mystical reaction ; so in England, those who failed to discover either in Puritanism or Anglicanism sufficient nourishment for their souls, became " seekers " after some more vivid expression of the spiritual life. This " search " was pursued along two main routes. On the one hand, the mystical poets Vaughan, Herbert, Traherne, and their contemporaries the Cambridge Platonists represent the path taken by various types of gentle, cultivated, moderately fervent—in fact, characteristically Anglican—spirits. Here we find much exquisite writing, much spiritual charm, but little evidence of first-hand struggle and experience. These, after all, are " tasters " rather than " seekers " of truth. We have only to compare the sugary Platonics of

Traherne, the pious rationalism of Whichcote, with the stern realism of Ruysbroeck, or even with Boehme's cloud and fire, to perceive that we have to do with a manufactured product of great beauty ; and not the strong raw stuff of actual life. The Platonists were highly cultivated and spiritually susceptible men. They knew and admired Plotinus, Dionysius the Areopagite, and many of the classics of mediæval mysticism ; which were at this period republished and widely read, influencing numerous religious writers who could not properly be described as mystics. But they show us, as St. Augustine had said long ago of their predecessors, " the vision of the land of peace—but not the road thereto."

The writings of Augustine Baker and his pupil Dame Gertrude More show another and more hopeful path taken by those who sought for a vivid experience of God ; but these represent the continuance and enrichment of traditional Catholic mysticism, not the contribution of the Protestant world. Within this Protestant world the number and variety of spiritual experiments attested the general unrest ; and many of these experiments were strongly influenced by Boehme's works. In Germany a sect of " Behmenists," rejecting the Christian ministry and sacraments, tried to perpetuate the master's teachings. In England Dr. Pordage (1608–98) and his associate, the apocalyptic visionary and prophetess, Jane Lead (1623–1704), reproduced Boehme's doctrine in its most confused and least fortunate form. Pordage, originally a clergyman, was deprived for heresy. His " sect " and the Philadelphian Society which sprang from it, together with the other theosophic, hermetic and illuminist groups of this uneasy period, faded away, leaving little of value behind.

It was not among any of these that the true revival of mystical religion was prepared. Alien from them, and also from the formalism of the official Church, there had grown up in all parts of England groups of spiritual " seekers " or " waiters "—a term first applied to them in 1617. Distinguished on one hand by a strong tendency to Quietism, on the other by belief in individual illumination and consequent hostility to external religion, these—as William Penn afterwards said of them—" left all visible churches and societies and wandered up and down as sheep without a shepherd . . . *seeking* their Beloved, but could not find Him as their souls desired to know Him." Influenced by the mystical and quietist literature which was now in general circulation, some practised great austerity of life and met regularly for silent prayer. Their importance in the history of the Church consists in the fact that they provided the spiritual landscape within which the mystical genius of George Fox (1624–91) developed ; and that the formation of the Society of Friends, that great experiment in corporate mysticism, largely represents their discovery, under his leadership, of the treasure they had sought.

Though it can hardly be contended that the Quaker method represents religion in its wholeness or ministers to all the complex needs of human souls, yet at least in its great period, and still in its greatest personalities, it witnesses to the mighty results that may be achieved by an uncompromising

Christian inwardness ; and shows how simple men and women may share the essential experiences of the contemplative life, and reach a first-hand apprehension of God inciting to heroic action and rivalling the conclusions of mystical philosophers. All this is ultimately derived from the spiritual creativeness of Fox himself, one of those great and life-giving personalities through whom from time to time the Spirit reaches out to men.

Fox, born of the craftsman class, and brought up in a strict but arid Puritan atmosphere, which could not satisfy his innate craving for spiritual reality, felt in adolescence the inward turmoil and longing for assurance so characteristic of religious genius of the " twice-born " type. At nineteen he left home and became in body as well as soul a "seeker"; for many of those to whom this name was given literally wandered over the country in their search for a spiritual home. " I was," he says, " a man of sorrows in the time of the first workings of the Lord in me." This period of conflict lasted for three years. It was brought to an end by the great and well-known ecstatic experience, comparable to those in which St. Augustine and St. Francis were born into new life, which gave him, once for all, absolute certitude.

> Then, O then, I heard a Voice which said, " There is one, even Christ Jesus, that can speak to thy condition "; and when I heard it, my heart did leap for joy . . . when God doth work, who shall let it ? And this I knew experimentally . . . and then the Lord did gently lead me along and did let me see His love, which was endless and eternal and surpasseth all the knowledge that men have in the natural state or can get by history or books.

In view of Fox's subsequent career, we cannot

doubt that this is the description of a genuine
mystical conversion, an opening of " the eye which
looks on eternity." It was indeed the first of
those "openings," or abrupt ecstatic apprehensions,
which witness to his abnormal psychic constitution
and supported his apostolic life. It was probably
in the following year that the establishment of his
consciousness on these new levels was completed
in a prolonged trance—said to have lasted fourteen
days—during which his whole bodily aspect became
changed ; and he afterwards declared that he had
been brought through " a very ocean of darkness
and death " into " the greatness and infinitude of
the Love of God which cannot be expressed in
words . . . an infinite ocean of light and love
which flowed over the ocean of darkness." These
phrases inevitably remind us of Boehme, whose
works were eagerly devoured by the early Quakers
and must have been known to Fox by the time
his *Journal* was composed ; and there are other
" openings " which approach even more closely
in character to Boehme's great pictorial intuitions
of Reality :

All things were new ; and all the creation gave another smell
unto me than before, beyond what words can utter . . . . The
creation was opened to me ; and it was showed me how all things
had their names given them, according to their nature and virtue.

Such passages, all belonging to his first period
of growth, prove Fox to have been a visionary ;
but it is the apostolic life which developed from
and through these experiences which gives him an
honoured place among the creative mystics of the
Church. In a period of arid religious formalism

he brought back, because he possessed it, the life-giving sense of the Presence of God. As St. Paul passed from the "abundance of revelations" to the strenuous career of itinerant missionary, and St. Teresa from the life of contemplation to the hard work of religious reform; so Fox's ecstatic openings prepared him for a wandering ministry which lasted forty years, often involved persecution, hardship and danger, and included visits to Holland, Germany, and Bermuda, and two years in America. Wherever he went he established groups of Friends, or as they were first called, "Children of the Light." With these disciples he remained in a close spiritual sympathy, sometimes even involving such a telepathic knowledge of their vicissitudes as St. Catherine of Siena had of her "sons." Uniting spiritual power with that stern common sense and capacity for detail so often found in the saints, he organized his groups with the thoroughness and success of a new St. Paul, colouring them with his own peculiar spirit and infecting them with his enthusiastic energy. His converts came from every class ; and his "first companions," like those of St. Francis, included the extremes of culture and simplicity.

With little education, and often rough and intolerant in manner, he is, nevertheless, an outstanding example of the "power of the Spirit" ; and there is much contemporary evidence of the immense impression which was made by his transfigured personality. Said William Penn of him : "The most awful, living, reverent frame I ever felt or beheld was his in prayer." An equivalent witness to that which would now be called his

" numinous " quality came from the Cambridge
students who had assembled to attack him, but
exclaimed " O hee shines, hee glisters ! " and let
him go unharmed—a story which should be com-
pared with the insistent and unexplained reports
of abnormal radiance which meet us in the lives of
earlier mystics. Nor was this enhancement of life
merely apparent. Attacked in 1652 by a mob,
and left for senseless on the ground, Fox himself
experienced the working of that healing gift which
he used on other men. " The power of the Lord
sprang through me," he said, " and the eternal
refreshings refreshed me," and to the astonish-
ment of his enemies he rose unharmed to his feet.
Yet more mysterious, this man, uninfluenced by
the mediæval ascetic traditions, felt that he was
called like certain Catholic saints to bear in his
own person the burden and grief of the world's
sins. " He bears the iniquity, wherever he comes,"
was said of him by one of his contemporaries.

Though it must be acknowledged that the
Quaker emphasis on inward experience alone, its
deliberate cult of quietistic devotion, and its complete rejection of external religion, means in practice a subtraction from the full human richness
of the Christian scheme, with its close interlocking
of inward and outward things ; yet plainly this
renewed emphasis on the invisible is one which is
perpetually needed if the realities of the spiritual
life are to survive.

In spite, then, of exaggerations in their doctrine,
Fox and his first companions must rank, as truly
as the first Franciscans, among the reconstructive
mystics of the Church. Their alienation from the

main Christian stream and wholesale rejection of its methods of worship, was an implied criticism of the Christian institutions which surrounded them; and we need not deny that these were at a low ebb. In a living Church their position need have differed little from that of Brother Lawrence ; for, had external forms still been found to convey spiritual value, the revolt from them would have been less intense. The extent to which a corporate mystical life, often of the deepest and purest kind, developed in the first Quaker communities is an indication that England, like France, was capable at this period of a genuine spiritual renaissance. But the English love of sects and passion for individualism and freedom, here replaced the Latin love of order, as the controlling factor in its outward expression.

Yet it is impossible to read the first-hand accounts of Quaker faith and life, based wholly on the principle of loving surrender and the " practice of the Presence of God," without perceiving the close identity between their fundamental ideas and those of the great saints of contemporary France. At many points the Quaker and the Catholic contemplative approach one another. It is significant that Quaker spirituality of the second generation was nourished, not only by the writings of Boehme and his precursors and followers, but also by the great masters of traditional mysticism, especially Thomas à Kempis and Fénelon. In these the Friends found those very principles that governed their own religious practice ; and through them they are linked with the great historic current of Christian spirituality.

SOME PROTESTANT MYSTICS

These writers fed the loving and courageous soul of John Woolman (1720–72); whose deep mystical consciousness of the unity in love of God and man drove him to vigorous and unpopular denunciations of slavery, and beyond this to a " concern " for the animal creation Franciscan in its tenderness and unique in his period and place.

I was early convinced (he says in his *Journal*) that true religion consisted in an inward life, wherein the Heart doth Love and Reverence God the Creator, and learn to exercise true Justice and Goodness, not only toward all men, but also toward the Brute Creatures. . . . That as by His breath the flame of life was kindled in all Animals and Sensible Creatures, to say we love God as unseen and at the same time exercise cruelty toward the least creature moving by His life, was a contradiction in itself.

This intense love of consistency, the determination that outward life and inward vision should be all of one piece, is a distinguishing character of Woolman's mysticism—the cause alike of his most heroic and most eccentric acts. In his deliberate linking-up of social questions with his interior vision of Divine Will and Love, he is indeed the first of the modern mystics; finding a close connection between the " pure Operation of the Holy Spirit " and " a longing in my mind that people might come into cleanness of spirit, cleanness of person, cleanness about their houses and garments."

Though he could say of himself that through " most steady attention to the voice of the True Shepherd . . . my Soul was so environed with Heavenly Light and Consolation that things were made easy to me which had been otherwise," he could not rest in this personal communion. It drove him to an ardent crusade against slavery, oppression, and the luxury of the propertied class, by which he earned the enmity of the rich American Quakers, exasperated by his constant demand for a return to the lost simplicity of the early Friends. " The weight of this degeneracy hath lain so heavy upon me," he says, " my heart has been so ardent for a reformation, that we may come to that right use of things where living on a little we may inhabit that holy Mountain in which they neither hurt nor destroy." Because of the miseries of the plantation slaves, he refused sugar ; because they were " stained with worldly glory " he would not use silver spoons ; because dyed cloth was " insincere " he wore undyed clothes—with the result that in spite of his real holiness " ye singularity of his appearance might in some Meetings Draw ye Attention of ye Youth, and even cause a change of Countenance in some." Yet these eccentricities all arose from the mystic's conviction of the sacramental character of outward things ; the mysterious unity of all life in God.

As Woolman's soul matured, his self-abandonment and austerities increased. Like Fox, he felt the call to take on himself the sorrows of the world. Of an experience which came to him two years before his death he says :

I saw a mass of matter of a dull gloomy colour, between the South and the East, and was informed that this mass was human beings, in as great misery as they could be, and live ; and that I was mixed in with them, and henceforth I might not consider myself as a distinct or separate being.

Surely here we find the link between the deep intuition of mystical union and those distinctively

Christian passions of pity and redemptive love which, in the last years of his devoted life, he poured without stint from his beloved " interior silence " on the needs and sorrows of all living things.

The light of true Quaker spirituality, at once so inward and so active, passed from Woolman to a succession of saintly and vigorous souls. It is seen again in Stephen Grellet (1773–1855), that untiring missionary of the Inward Light, and in the heroic prison-reformer Elizabeth Fry (1780–1845), who found in the silence that mysterious power which " loves the unlovely into loveableness." These convince us of the continuously life-giving character of that Spirit which George Fox served and proclaimed.

Though the influence of Jacob Boehme is most marked in the Quakers, and other sectarian promoters of religious inwardness, and later in the quite unchurched mysticism of Blake (1757–1827), that powerful genius also contributed something to the revival of mysticism in the Anglican Church. Through the interpretations of his great disciple William Law (1686–1761) his teachings brought their renewing touch to English institutionalism at one of the most deadly moments of its career. William Law's few mystical writings were produced in the later part of his life ; for Boehme's influence reached him in middle age. Belonging to the High Church party, and having small sympathy with the religious rationalism of the Cambridge Platonists, the " inward light " of God's prevenient and all-penetrative presence is as central to Law's teaching as it is to that of the Quakers. " There is but one salvation for all mankind, and that is the Life of God in the soul . . . you have no true religion, are no worshipper of the one true God, but in and by that Spirit of Love which is God Himself living and working in you." " Turn therefore inwards, and all that is within you will demonstrate to you the Presence and Power of God in your soul, and make you find and feel it, with the same certainty as you find and feel your own thoughts."

It is this vivid, unflinching realism, this demand for a true organic life and growth of the spirit, founded on a change in the direction of its will and desire—for he equals St. Augustine in his insistence on the will as " the only workman in nature "—which gives to Law's mystical writings their freshness and stimulating power. He learned from Boehme the way to a vastly enriched and deepened vision of God, and His relation with the soul ; and in the light of that vision was able to give expression to the ancient truths of Christian mysticism. We cannot doubt that he experienced that interior transformation which he passionately proclaims ; and which turned the brilliant ecclesiastic into the gentle and saintly recluse and director of souls, who wrote *The Spirit of Love* and *The Spirit of Prayer*. Through these little books, into which Law poured the fruits of his deep musings and his secret communion with God, he has influenced, and continues to influence, many souls. He was read and appreciated by the leaders of the Evangelical Revival ; and the mystical element in that movement owes something to its contact through him with the great traditional doctrines of the interior life.

SOME PROTESTANT MYSTICS

Since the Evangelical Revival was mainly a return to religious realism, and especially to that ardent personal devotion which has always formed one strand in the Church's secret life, we might expect to find in it a nursery of mystics. This, notoriously, it did not become. Nevertheless, in the greatest souls whom it nourished, we see again the special quality of sanctity, tender, childlike, heroic, and contagious, which is the characteristic product of Christocentric mysticism. In Henry Martyn (1781–1812) we have a typical and beautiful example of its transforming power. A study of this half-forgotten scholar-mystic, who, in an atmosphere even hostile to the ideals of Catholicism, was possessed of the same experience, and driven to the same disciplines, as the mystics of the mediæval Church, may well complete our survey of Protestant mysticism. Here we may realize its substantial identity with the classic Christian expressions of spiritual life.

Born at Truro, and growing up in a religious atmosphere coloured by Wesley's influence, Martyn was a brilliant, hypersensitive, unstable, not specially religious boy. His conversion took place at Cambridge, and was chiefly due to the influence of Charles Simeon. Simeon, a generation older than Martyn—mystical, passionately Christocentric, full of energy, courting persecution for the sake of his ideals—was one of the great apostolic souls of the Evangelical movement. Martyn, though a Wesleyan background and the immense impression made upon him by the life of David Brainerd counted for much in his development, is essentially his spiritual child.

THE MYSTICS OF THE CHURCH

With an intellect of exceptional power and delicacy, now doubled by a growing spiritual sense, Martyn is an outstanding example of that well-marked saintly type to which his French contemporary Jean-Nicholas Grou (1731–1803), mystic and Platonist, and later the holy and scholarly Abbé Huvelin (1839–1910) also belonged : a type in which the activities of an exquisite and critical mind are combined with a childlike, humble, and adoring attitude of soul. At twenty-one he was Senior Wrangler, and assured of a brilliant academic career. Two years later he was ordained, and under the dominion of his growing desire to help and redeem, was struggling as one of Charles Simeon's curates with the pastoral duties most alien to his shy and fastidious temperament. He had now begun, too, that impassioned study of Oriental languages in which, for the rest of his life, he found interest and refreshment. More significant still, he, a child of the most rigidly Protestant piety, began to discipline his body by those physical austerities which possess such undying attraction for the saints. In 1805, drawn to further renunciations, he sailed for India as a missionary chaplain. Only the spiritual journal kept during these years reveals his true life, and the springs of action which dictated his sacrifices. We see in its successive entries the growth of his soul, its deepening and expanding experience of God.

My imagination takes to itself wings and flies to some wilderness where I may hold converse in solitude with God. . . . What is this world, what is religious company, what is anything to me without God ? They become a bustle and a crowd when I lose sight of Him. The most dreary wilderness would appear Paradise with a little of His presence. . . . I had such need of being alone with God. . . . It sometimes appeared astonishing that men of like passions with myself, of the same bodies, alike in every other respect, knew and saw nothing of that blest and adorable Being in whom my soul findeth all its happiness.

These extracts date from his academic period, when he had to bear the ridicule and contempt which his intellectual equals reserved for those who took religion seriously. During the physical hardships and intense spiritual loneliness of the nine months' journey to India, in pastoral charge of a ship's company of the roughest type, a manifest deepening of his mystical life took place. Not only the joys of contemplative experience—" the transcendent sweetness of the privilege of being always with God would appear to me *too* great, were it not for the blessed command, ' Set your affections on things above ' "—but a new consciousness of something far greater, more authoritative than these emotional delights, now came to him : " I perceived for the first time the difference between sensible sweetness in religion, and the really valuable attainments."

Thus the man who reached Calcutta in 1806 had already achieved something like spiritual maturity : a fact soon recognized by those capable of appreciating it. During the remaining six years of his life his growth was the saint's growth in outflowing love, simplicity, devotedness. In the touching descriptions of his desperate but often unavailing efforts to teach and win souls, and of the contagious influence of his own spirit of selfless love, we rediscover the methods, longings, and achievements of all the apostolic mystics of the Church, from Francis of Assisi to the Quaker saints. " I wish," said Martyn, " to have my whole soul swallowed up in the Will of God " ; and we seem to see the fulfilment of this desire through the reports of his contemporaries. " The outbeaming of his soul," said one who knew him, " would absorb the attention of every observer " ; and another, " he shines in all the dignity of love, and seems to carry about him such a heavenly majesty, as impresses the mind beyond description."

Yet he combined this spiritual ascendancy with that wide and supple power of entering fully and simply into each phase and moment of life, which is the crowning grace of those who are really at home with God. He could turn from the uphill pastoral labours of an Anglo-Indian chaplain of that day to his great and absorbing work of translating the New Testament into Hindustani, Arabic, and Persian—a task in which nothing satisfied him which fell below the level of the most exact scholarship—and from this again to delighted intercourse with the children or animals by whom he was always adored. " A little dog to play with, or what would be best of all a dear little child," were the companions he longed for when his health broke down. His friends worshipped him as a saint : to others he was " a learned and cheerful man."

The last years of Martyn's short and various life have a heroic and romantic character which link him with such great missionary mystics as St. Francis Xavier, whom he so greatly admired and envied, and the intrepid saint of the Sahara,

Charles de Foucauld. Driven by ill-health from India, he could not rest, but travelled with much difficulty to Persia, that he might get his translation of the Scriptures revised by Persian scholars. We have in his letters a vivid and amazing picture of his life in Shiraz ; the gentle, studious, and fragile Evangelical clergyman, now disguised in Persian dress and adopting local manners, but still " singing hymns over my milk and water," since " tea I have none." Alone amongst a hostile Moslem population, to whom he fearlessly preached the Christian faith, he was yet " clothed in an almost magical calm " ; and was recognized by the more spiritual amongst them as belonging to the universal company of the saints. Deep conversations took place between the Christian missionary and the Sūfi mystics, whom he quaintly described as " the Methodists of the East." " I am sometimes led on," he said, " to tell them all I know of the very recesses of the sanctuary ; and these are the things that interest them." The " love clear, sweet and strong " which glorified and supported Martyn's sufferings and efforts here transcended credal barriers, and revealed one to another these diverse seekers for an identical Reality. His task finished, he started for England in a dying condition ; and after a journey marked by the extremes of physical misery and spiritual joy died in great loneliness at Tokat, aged only thirty-one.

ILLUSTRATIVE WORKS

Boehme, Jacob. The Aurora. Translated by J. Sparrow. London, 1914.

Six Theosophic Points. Translated by J. R. Earle. London, 1919.

The Way to Christ. London, 1911.

Confessions of. Edited by W. Scott Palmer. London, 1920.

Braithwaite, W. The Beginnings of Quakerism. London, 1912.

Christian Life, Faith, and Thought, being the first Part of the Book of Christian Discipline of the Religious Society of Friends. London, 1922.

Emmott, E. B. A Short History of Quakerism. London, 1923.

Fox, George. Journal. Edited from the MSS. by N. Penney. Cambridge, 1911.

Jones, Rufus. Spiritual Reformers in the 16th and 17th Centuries. London, 1914.

Law, William. Liberal and Mystical Writings. Edited by W. Scott Palmer. London, 1908.

Padwick, C. Henry Martyn, Confessor of the Faith. London, 1922.

Woolman, John. Journal and Essays. Edited by A. M. Gummere. London, 1922.

CHAPTER XII

CONCLUSION : MODERN MYSTICS

GIOSUE BORSI—J. W. ROWNTREE—LUCIE-CHRISTINE—
CHARLES DE FOUCAULD—SADHU SUNDAR SINGH

IT is a curious fact that those who study and admire
the great mystics of Christendom, constantly assume
that their experiences belong wholly to the past :
that " modern mystics," if they exist at all, must
be of another species, and express their desire for
God in other ways. Yet if the Church be indeed
a living and enduring fact, a true organism, the
mystical element of her corporate life must also
endure, and bring from time to time its gift of
supernatural joy and certitude to the common store.
Moreover, such a mystical element will retain
certain unchanging characteristics, since it arises
in the soul's experience of the Unchanging God.
Its outward expression may vary : its substance
will always be the same. This we have indeed
learnt in our survey of the Christian centuries :
St. Paul joins hands with Henry Martyn, and the
period between is filled with men and women who
share the same vision, life and power, accept,
enrich and carry on the same traditions and speak
the same native language of the soul.

It is less easy to show the continuance of this
tradition when we come to our own times. Those
whose experience is deepest will be least inclined to

reveal it, save indirectly, to the world. "My secret to myself" will always remain true, at least in some degree, of the real mystic; whose contemporaries can only guess at the nature of his hidden life by its results. The fact that certain published works of so-called "modern mystics" disappoint us by their crude quietism, their shallow volubility, or their un-Christian claim to an exclusive and aristocratic intimacy with God, need not involve the pessimistic belief that the Church can no longer bear and nourish souls capable of a direct and life-giving experience of His richness and love. In every period the number of hidden saints must immensely exceed those whose records are preserved ; and even those immediately concerned with spiritual work cannot fully know the amount of genuine mysticism now existing, the numbers of men and women whose lives are centred upon conscious communion with God.

Yet here and there in contemporary literature we find direct evidence that this same life is being lived, this same development is taking place ; that surrender still issues in spiritual power. Those who read the human and beautiful diary called *A Soldier's Confidences with God*—written partly in the trenches by a young Italian officer during the Great War, and discovered after his heroic death— could not doubt that here they saw the first, ardent, yet sometimes hesitating, steps of a spirit called to the path of the mystical saints. Even making full allowance for the patent influence of St. Augustine, Dante and Pascal, we find here one who had a genuine share in their spirit of penitence and adoring love, and knew something of their deep

experience. Here the classic Catholic tradition
of the spiritual life once more proves its vitality.
It is accepted and re-expressed by a completely
modern spirit : a brilliant young man of the world,
a poet and scholar, brought up in an anti-clerical
atmosphere, yet deeply aware of God's prevenient
action, both inspiring and demanding the generous
co-operation of his soul.

> Thou art speaking to me directly ; my heart is filled with Thee,
> all at once, entirely and without effort ! I feel Thee in me, Thou art
> speaking to me : " Courage, My beloved son, courage, for I love thee
> and I want thee ; fear no more, hesitate no longer, cast off the last
> hawsers, launch forth into the sea, and turn not back even for a glance."

Along another line, John Wilhelm Rowntree,
the Quaker (1868–1905), continues the same direct
spiritual realism ; in the form in which it inspired
the early Friends, and upheld his own life when
he was threatened with early blindness. He has
told the story of how, leaving the consultation at
which this sentence was pronounced, he " suddenly
felt the love of God wrap him about as though a
visible presence enfolded him, and a joy filled him
such as he had never known before." And in
another passage he speaks less directly, yet in
terms plainly dependent on a deep personal experience, of " the whole soul flooded with light and
love . . . the unspeakable peace " experienced by
those whom we might call mystics of the Pauline
type, for whom the Christian vision and the
Christian life are merged in one, adding :

> " I have sketched, you say, a hypothetical career. No, it is a
> story from real life. You say I have spoken in mystical language.
> I answer, Yes, the supreme moment cannot be defined in the dry
> language of theology, nor can words express it. You say the

experience is the result of mental suggestion practised over a term of years. I answer, No one believes that who has once been there and taken off his shoes on holy ground—the reality is too over-powering, the effect too profound . . ."

Testimonies of this kind might be—and as time goes on doubtless will be—multiplied indefinitely. Those already made public are enough to prove the identity and continuity of the Christian mystical experience. The secret lives of hard-bitten missionaries and explorers such as David Livingstone (1813–73) or the Vicomte de Foucauld ; of devoted women such as Mother Janet Stuart (1857–1914) or Mary Slessor (1848–1915), who have performed apparently superhuman works in the spirit and strength of prayer ; or of cloistered contemplatives such as Elizabeth de la Trinité (1880–1906) and the newly-canonized Thérèse de l'Enfant Jésus (1873–97) ; or of converts from agnosticism such as Madeleine Sémer (1874–1921), mysteriously initiated into the experiences of the saints, all disclose the same power and attraction at work—an attraction and power identical with that revealed in the New Testament. Three widely differing personalities of our own time, whose mystical experience in its depth, vigour and transforming power, can bear comparison with the classic standards of mysticism, may serve as illustrations of this truth. The first is the lady whose *Spiritual Journal* was published after her death under the pseudonym of Lucie-Christine (1844–1908) ; the next is the " hermit of the Sahara," the heroic Charles de Foucauld (1858–1916) ; the last—still living—the Indian convert and missionary, Sadhu Sundar Singh.

Lucie-Christine was a Frenchwoman of the

leisured class, who married when she was twenty-
one and became the devoted mother of five children.
The circumstances of her life, like those of Madame
Acarie, contradict the idea that the mystical vocation involves the neglect or the absence of ordinary
human duties and relationships, or a deliberate
retirement from the world. Indeed, her interest
for us largely consists in the discovery that this
deeply affectionate, sensitive, and intelligent woman,
whose one desire was to "appear ordinary," who
was often absorbed in home duties and willingly
took part in social life, was continually possessed
by a secret experience of God identical in character
and comparable in richness with that of the great
mystics. She entered completely into her children's
interests and amusements, wrote and staged the
plays which they acted, welcomed their friends ;
fought and conquered her natural desire for solitude, and distaste for the trivial details and inter-
ruptions of daily life. Yet, once alone, " my soul
found itself transported into the Infinity of God ; not
merely as into some new region, but as if, having
lost its own life, it was living in the Infinite itself."

When Lucie-Christine's contemplative life first
developed, she knew nothing of the writings of the
mystics ; and was ignorant of the very names of
those degrees of prayer and union, those vivid
intuitions of God, which she describes with such
delicacy and freshness. She therefore guarantees
to us, as few of the traditional mystics have done,
the objective reality of these experiences : their
independence of the suggestions inherent in mediæval religion. To the world she appeared only a
fervent and exact Christian of the French Catholic
type, with a special devotion to the Eucharist.

Her friends realized in her a growing beauty of soul, a strange peace-giving power, a silent influence which more than once brought unbelievers to God. But it was only after her death that the journal which she had kept for many years at the wish of her spiritual director and confidant disclosed the range and beauty of a mystical experience which places this unassuming woman in the spiritual family of Julian of Norwich, Angela of Foligno and St. Teresa.

Lucie-Christine was by nature deeply religious, and there is no trace of anything which we can call a conversion in her experiences. But her initiation into the mystical life, which took place when she was nearly thirty years of age, was abrupt and apparently unprepared.

"This morning," she says, "I was making my meditation on the 'Imitation of Christ,' as I have been accustomed to do this last thirteen years, when suddenly I saw before my inward eyes these words—*God Alone*. It is strange to say that one sees words, yet it is certain that I see and hear them inwardly, but not in the ordinary manner of sight and hearing; and further I feel how badly my words express that which I experienced, although the remembrance has remained very vivid to me. It was at the same time a Light, an Attraction and a Power. A Light which showed me how I could belong completely to God alone in the world, and I saw that hitherto I had not well understood this; an Attraction, by which my heart was subdued and delighted; a Power which inspired me with a generous resolution, and in some way placed in my hands the means of carrying it out; for it is the property of these Divine words to do what they say: and these were the first that God vouchsafed to let my soul hear, and His mercy made them the starting point of a new life. But lo! my God, I have undertaken to tell of Thy inward works, and from the first I feel that words fail me. It seems to me that they do not exist to tell of such things. . . . And since it is to obey Thee that I write, do Thou take care that I fall not into any fault, and give Thy poor little creature means of expressing that which is so far above natural comprehension."

From this moment of revelation to the end of her life Lucie-Christine's existence was centred on a vivid consciousness of God's Presence, "its invisible and irresistible charm," which grew in intensity as time went on, clothing and inundating her as she went about her domestic duties, pressing her to "perform every little daily act with love." Sometimes this awareness forsook her, and she passed through those periods of desolation and obscurity which are the price that all the mystics pay for their happiness ; but more often the Divine companionship so filled her with rapture that she found it hard to conceal her ecstatic joy.

My way is very simple. My soul lives on God, by a glance of love between Him and herself. By this glance God gives Himself to me, and I give myself to Him. This is my habitual state, that in which God has placed me. I neither can nor should turn myself from it on account of suffering. This I accept as inseparable from love here below. Love suffers as the voice sings. . . .

For two days now God gives me each time that I go into church a sense of His Presence that I cannot express, finding it above all ideas. It is a full sight, although it has no form ; it is at the same time sight and union. I am plunged in God. I see Him so intensely that my soul is more certain and more possessed by the sight than my bodily eyes by the light of day ; and at the same time He is in me, He is one with me, penetrates me, is closer to me than the air I breathe, is more united to me than the soul is united to the body which lives by it ; I am absorbed by Him. I no longer know by what existence I exist, it seems to me that I am transported into another life, a region that is no more this earth ; and this detachment is ineffable, it is a rapture and inebriation. Therein the soul knows God as no speech could make Him known to her, and there results from this an ardent thirst to abase all other souls before Him.

THE MYSTICS OF THE CHURCH

These passages, taken almost at random from her *Journal*, put beyond doubt Lucie-Christine's right to a place among the mystics of the Church. Though it might seem at first sight as though the creative side of the full mystical life was but slightly developed in her, and her deep union with God had few results upon the outer world, yet time has proved her to be one of those of whom her contemporary, the saintly Abbé Huvelin, has said that " they do good by what they are, rather than by what they do." " I have sought," she said, " how I might make God more loved by other souls, how to make apparent to them that gentleness and sweetness, that unspeakable peace . . . how obey the Holy Spirit, the fire which I feel in my soul and which desires to give itself, how communicate to all souls that which touches my soul : and I have not found any other or more powerful way than kindness."

But beyond this quiet and penetrative influence, her *Journal* has proved to thousands of readers how perfect a life of prayer and contemplation is possible to men and women fulfilling all the duties of normal human life ; how untrue it is that the deepest knowledge of God is the prerogative of a special class, or the reward of those who have stifled their natural affections. She witnesses, too, to the intimate connection between visible and invisible religion ; passing easily and with no sense of contrast from formal and liturgic to formless and silent adoration, and finding as her spiritual life develops ever more truth and meaning in the great doctrines of the Church.

Her mystical range was wide : on one side

passionately Christocentric, she was yet capable of those great metaphysical apprehensions "wherein there is no duration, neither past nor future, but one moment unique and infinite " which are characteristic of the highest states of contemplation : that sense of the timeless Being of God " so absolutely other than that which we know, that when He manifests Himself to the soul, the soul cannot doubt that it is Himself." Few among the historic mystics, and none among the modern, can rival her power of communicating this certitude. The trials and bereavements of her life, and the many years of increasing blindness in which it closed, did nothing to darken that " simple and evident sight."

" Where all reasoning fails," she says in such a time of overwhelming sorrow, " where the soul is so troubled that she could not even explain that which troubles her, there the Divine Presence appears ; and suddenly the dizziness ceases, and peace is re-born with light."

No more complete contrast could be imagined than that between Lucie-Christine and her contemporary, the Vicomte Charles de Foucauld. Her mystical experience was the flower of a completely Christian life ; his, of the penitence and self-immolation of a great convert. If she speaks only in her writings, he does chiefly in his deeds. If her external life was commonplace and lacking in incident, his was one of the most strange and romantic known to the modern world.

A lazy, arrogant, and self-indulgent boy, Foucauld lost his faith whilst still adolescent ; and for thirteen years was alienated from religion. Entering the army, he was known as an agreeable but in-

tensely indolent young man, a dilettante in literature, and a lover of good food. He was dismissed
his regiment for immorality. In 1882, when he
was twenty-four, came the French campaign in
Algeria. Then, suddenly, this naturally adventurous spirit awoke to the realities of life ; and
this, his first real call to action, effected a moral
though not religious conversion. He returned to
the army, accepted with delight the hardships of
desert life, was careless of his own safety, but
infinitely careful of and beloved by his men. The
following year he undertook that pioneer journey
into the interior of Morocco, which places him
among the greatest African explorers. Disguised
as a Moroccan Jew, he wandered for eleven months
in constant danger, penetrating to cities where no
European dared go. In 1885 he made a four
months' exploration of the South Algerian desert;
drawn there by that growing passion for solitude,
silence, and the simplification of life, which afterwards decided his religious vocation.

It seems to have been during these lonely journeys
that his thoughts first turned towards God : influenced by the sense of contrast between his own
attitude and that of the Mohammedan population,
who referred all things instinctively to Him, and
whose lives were punctuated by times of prayer.
Returning in 1886 to Paris, celebrated and admired
but inwardly without peace, Foucauld met the
Abbé Huvelin : that remarkable maker of saints
who did not merely teach, but *was* religion, and
who had sacrificed a brilliant career in scholarship
in order to become the curate of a small Parisian
church because he " desired to write in souls."

Foucauld, still without faith and with a sinful past, found himself in the presence of a fellow-man, outwardly genial, secretly austere, his equal in energy and intellect ; a man who had been transformed into the very spirit of holiness, and whose life was one act of prayer and compassion for the weakness and suffering of men. The impression was profound. Within a few weeks of their meeting, he had made his submission to Huvelin, and was received back into the Church.

The complete self-giving to anything he undertook, the disregard of personal comfort, the astonishing power of endurance, which had made of Foucauld a great explorer, was now poured into the religious channel. Years afterwards he revealed that upon the day following his conversion, he felt himself called by Christ to imitate His life of poverty and lowliness, and accepted this vocation without reserve. After a voyage to the Holy Land, he determined on a religious career and entered the Trappist order ; the most severe life which the Catholic Church can now offer her sons. During the six years which he spent as a monk—chiefly in the poor monastery of Akbès in Syria—the converted adventurer grew swiftly in spiritual power. " God makes me find in the solitude and silence a consolation on which I had not counted. I am constantly, absolutely constantly, with Him and with those I love." At Akbès, he soon came to be regarded as a saint. " He did not believe— he *saw*," said one who knew him there. Austere, but never ailing, he seemed to live without difficulty on a minimum of food and sleep impossible to other men.

But even this life of self-immolation could not satisfy him. He craved a greater humiliation and loneliness ; and finally, obtaining release from his order, went to Nazareth. There, in imitation of the hidden life of Christ, he lived for three years in abject poverty in the garden of the convent of the Poor Clares, from whom, in exchange for work, he received his food. All spare time was given to prayer and study ; St. John Chrysostom, St. Teresa, and St. John of the Cross being the authors on whom he formed his soul. The brilliant and self-indulgent aristocrat, the celebrated explorer, now had the position of an odd-job man and the appearance of a tramp; but a tramp whose whole being was irradiated with love and peace, since he possessed "a union with God in every instant—in prayer, reading, work, everything."

In 1900, on the advice of his religious superiors, Foucauld went to Rome to study for the priest-hood ; and the next year fulfilled his deepest desire—to return, as a missionary hermit, to those deserts of North Africa which he so deeply loved. During the retreat which he made at his ordination he felt his pastoral call to be to "the most sick sheep, the most forsaken souls " ; and, knowing no people so abandoned as the tribes of the Algerian Sahara, he determined to live among them in complete poverty, spreading the Gospel not by word of mouth but by life. His attitude was simply and literally apostolic. Invited to return as a priest to the Holy Land, he answered : " One must not go where the land is most holy, but where souls are in greatest need."

After three solitary years in his tiny hermitage

or " Fraternity " at Beni Abbès—he loved to call himself the "universal brother "—the old passion of the explorer reinforced the enthusiasms of the saint. In utter loneliness, for all his efforts to persuade others to join in a life of such austerity had failed, he pushed south to Tamanrasset in the Sahara. Here he lived as a hermit among the Touareg tribes, until his assassination in 1916. So gentle, loving, and good-humoured were the manners of this ferocious ascetic and advanced contemplative, that these fanatical and suspicious Mohammedans soon came to love him; as the most irreligious soldiers of the Beni Abbès garrison had done. Recognizing in him a " holy man," they called him the "Marabout Charles," came to him in all their troubles, and nursed him when he fell ill.

Like Henry Martyn, Grou, and other scholar-mystics, Foucauld knew the importance of mental discipline for the healthy life of the soul ; and worked steadily in his solitude at a dictionary of the Tamachek language and other tasks. He also brought his keen intelligence and special experience to bear on the problem of the conversion of the North African peoples ; best effected, he thought, by the gradual penetration among them of persons leading Christian lives of charity and prayer. " I ought to do the best I can for the souls of these infidels, in complete forgetfulness of self." And the means he found best were the purely spiritual energies—prayer, penitence, good example, kindness, personal sanctification—" using these myself, and doing my very best to increase the number of those using them."

The mystical side of his life was deeply hidden,

and recognized chiefly by its outward effects. But the meditations and letters which were published after his death reveal something of that profound and realistic sense of Divine Companionship, which made solitude the greatest of delights to him and found its chief outward expression in the Eucharist ; for he was above all else a Sacramental and Christocentric mystic.

"When we love (he wrote to his sister) we live less in ourselves than in that which we love; and the more we love, the more we establish our life beyond ourselves in that which we love." And to a friend, from his desert hermitage, " I am in great inward peace : do not worry because I am alone, without a friend or any spiritual support. I do not suffer from this solitude—I find it very sweet. I have the Blessed Sacrament. . . . I am happy and lack nothing." And in a letter written on December 1st, 1916, only a few hours before his martyrdom, " When one can suffer and love one can do much : one can do the utmost that is possible in this world. We feel when we suffer—we do not always feel when we love ; and this is a great added suffering. But we know that we want to love ; and to want to love is to love ! "

The contribution made by such a life as this to the corporate treasure of the Church, cannot of course be measured by its outward accomplishment. It is an easy task for common sense to discount Foucauld's career. His actual converts were few ; though probably none with whom he came in contact was unaffected by his spirit of humility and love. But his real work, like that of Lucie-Christine, has been done among those whom he never saw, and to whom his career has proved that the love of God has still the power to inspire lives of heroic sacrifice and self-abandonment, comparable with those which shame and astonish us in the histories of the saints.

MODERN MYSTICS

Our last example of this continuing energy, the Sadhu Sundar Singh, is well known to all English students of religious experience. Since he is still living, we cannot of course obtain here a perspective view of his spiritual course. We can only observe in a new setting those characteristics which we have been studying in his spiritual ancestors. It is not only from the point of view of tradition that the Sadhu interests us. As the first Indian mystic of the Christocentric type, he has an importance of his own. He was brought up from childhood within an ancient religious culture, which accepted without question the reality of God, and the soul's need of Him. As a boy he was trained in Yoga, the classic discipline of Indian contemplatives ; thus learning that art of concentration which has served him well in his Christian life. But Hindu theism, even at its best, failed to satisfy his thirst for personal communion with God : whilst for Christianity he felt, like the unconverted Paul, nothing but abhorrence. His conversion, which took place with startling suddenness when he was sixteen and his religious unrest was at its height, inevitably reminds us of that of the great apostle. He had been praying, almost in despair, for an assurance of God, when—

At 4.30 a.m. I saw something of which I had no idea at all previously. In the room where I was praying I saw a great light. I thought the place was on fire. I looked round, but could find nothing. Then the thought came to me that this might be an answer God had sent me. Then as I prayed and looked into the light, I saw the form of the Lord Jesus Christ. . . . The thought then came to me, Jesus Christ is not dead but living and it must be He Himself. So I fell at His feet and got this wonderful Peace which I could not get anywhere else.

He was soon called to suffer for his faith. His family, wealthy Sikhs hostile to Christianity, tried first to coerce, then to poison him ; finally casting him out to utter poverty. He became a Christian Sadhu or "holy man," devoted to prayer and meditation, wandering from village to village, and depending on alms : thus adapting a religious institution of India to the purposes of Christianity, and reproducing in an Oriental setting the wandering missionary life of St. Francis—for whom he has a deep admiration—and of Richard Rolle. Like St. Francis, he has remained a lay missionary; an attempt to train for orders proving conclusively how alien were his vision and temper from the ecclesiastical side of modern Christianity. In religious organization he takes no interest whatever. He does not feel impelled to gather a group of disciples or found a Church ; and the mutual exclusiveness of the various Christian bodies is incomprehensible to him. "The children of God are very dear but very queer—very nice but very narrow," he said as he withdrew to the undenominational position he firmly maintains.

The truth is that the Sadhu's mystical life springs from a source which lies far beyond theological controversies. It is essentially a reproduction of the direct and personal mysticism of the New Testament; continuing the Pauline tradition of first-hand communion with the exalted Christ. Perhaps so perfect a return to primitive conditions is now impossible to any mystic born within the Christian fold ; indeed to any Western mind. The freshness and ease with which St. Paul's great declarations are actualized by this the latest of his spiritual descendants, are partly the result of the affinity between the Oriental soul and an Oriental faith. The great contribution made by Sundar Singh to the mystical experience of the Church, consists in this demonstration that where the necessary conditions are present the most mysterious promises of the Gospel are still literally fulfilled ; and it is this which makes him so appropriate a figure with whom to end our survey of the mystics of the Church.

The Sadhu's experience, like that of St. Paul, is not only Christocentric but ecstatic. He claims an abundance of " visions and revelations " from which he brings back new knowledge of the spiritual world, and new vitality and power. He speaks in Pauline terms—though never publicly—of the truths revealed to him in that " Third Heaven " where all things pour forth adoration, and " no one hides their love or what is in their heart."

Often when I come out of ecstasy I think the whole world must be blind not to see what I see, everything is so near and so clear . . . there is no language which will express the things which I see and hear in the spiritual world.

Yet a homely sense of Divine indwelling balances these transcendental apprehensions. If the Third Heaven is ineffable, the First Heaven is that inward peace and joy which he expects to find in every Christian's heart as in his own. " I said, ' Where is the capital of Heaven ? Where He is sitting ? ' They told me, ' No, in every heart that loves Him.' " This experience is supported by the daily periods of prayer and meditation—never less than two, often four hours or more—which the Sadhu considers as necessary as breathing to his life. It inspires, moreover, an active, and even an adventurous career. In addition to religious work in India, he makes dangerous missionary journeys in Tibet and the Himalaya, has endured persecution, and escaped by apparent miracle from death. Thus, perhaps depending less than any of the historical mystics on the literature and tradition of the Church—the Bible and the " Imitation of Christ " are the only books which have greatly influenced him—he has arrived by his own path at a spiritual outlook and experience, a two-fold relationship with God, substantially identical with that of the great family of Christian contemplatives. Like them, he lives the balanced life of work and contemplation, and seems able to infect others with his own intense consciousness of God. Hence he witnesses in our own day as clearly as the saints of earlier centuries, to the actuality of that Power and Experience which make of the great Christian mystics " the life-giving members of Holy Church."

ILLUSTRATIVE WORKS

Bazin, R.   Charles de Foucauld.   London, 1923.
Borsi, G.   A Soldier's Confidences with God.   New York, 1918.
Klein, F.   Madeleine Sémer, Convertie et Mystique. 16th edition.   Paris, 1924.
Lucie-Christine.   Spiritual Journal ot.   London, 1915.
Rowntree, J. W.   Man's Relation to God.   London, 1917.
Streeter, B. H. and A. J. Appasamy.   The Sadhu : a Study in Mysticism and Practical Religion.   London, 1921.

INDEX

INDEX

Elijah, 30
Elizabeth de la Trinité, 242
Elizabeth of Schonau, 79
Evangelical Revival, 210, 232 *seq.*

Fénelon, 24, 191, 209 *seq.*, 228
Fitch, W., 189
Foucauld, Charles de, 237, 242, 247 *seq.*
Fox, George, 223 *seq.*
Francis Borgia, St., 171
Franciscan Mysticism, 92 *seq.*, 111, 172, 190, 221
    Spirituals, 94, 137
    Tertiaries, 95, 101
Francis de Sales, St., 190 *seq.*, 196 *seq.*
Francis of Assisi, St., 33, 37, 90 *seq.*, 110, 115, 254
    Stigmata, 93
Francis Xavier, St., 236
Friends of God, 137 *seq.*, 147
Fry, Elizabeth, 231

Gertrude, St., 79 *seq.*
Gnostics, 55
Grace, 48
Grellet, Stephen, 231
Grou, J. N., 234, 251
Guyon, Madame, 187, 191
    Life, 207 *seq.*

Helfde, 79 *seq.*
Herbert, George, 221
Hildegarde, St., 74 *seq.*, 137, 153
Hilton, Walter, 23, 114, 123 *seq.*
Holy Name, Cult of, 24, 88, 112, 115, 127
Hugh of St. Victor, 121
Huvelin, Abbé, 100, 234, 246, 248 *seq.*

Ignatius, St., 152, 168 *seq.*
    Spiritual Exercises, 170

Illumination, 27, 43, 103, 150, 214, 218
Isaiah, 31 *seq.*

Jacopone da Todi, 92, 95 *seq.*, 109, 221
    Poems of, 96 *seq.*
Jeremiah, 34
Jesuits, 171
Jesus Christ, 23 *seq.*, 29, 36 *seq.*
Jesu dulcis memoria, 88, 111
John of Avila, 172
John of La Verna, 94
John of the Cross, St., 169, 172
    Life, 181 *seq.*
    Writings, 183
Juan de los Angeles, 169
Julian of Norwich, 106, 110, 113, 124, 127 *seq.*, 160, 215

La Combe, Père, 209
Lawrence, Brother, 189 *seq.*, 200 *seq.*
Law, William, 219, 231 *seq.*
Lead, Jane, 222
Livingstone, David, 242
Lucie-Christine, 242 *seq.*
Luther, 212

Malaval, 207
Marguerite Acarie, Mère, 194
Marie de l'Incarnation, 190, 202 *seq.*
Martyn Henry, 233 *seq.*, 251
Mechthild of Hackeborn, St., 79 *seq.*
Mechthild of Magdeburg, 79 *seq.*
Merswin, Rulman, 138
Mohammed, 11
Molinos, 207
Monasticism, Early, 56 *seq.*
Monica, St., 64, 66
Montanists, 55
More, Dame Gertrude, 204, 222

INDEX

Mystical theology, 15, 81
   types, 15 *seq.*
Mysticism, defined, 9 *seq.*, 20
   Bible, 30 *seq.*
   Christocentric, 23 *seq.*, 39, 111,
     124, 133, 206, 233, 247, 252,
     255
   English, 112
   Flemish, 133 *seq.*
   Franciscan, 93, 190
   French, 188
   German, 136
   and history, 17 *seq.*, 30
   Personal, 20 *seq.*, 254
   and sacramentalism, 21, 24, 149,
     162, 166, 244, 252
   Spanish, 168
   Theocentric, 23 *seq.*, 68, 134,
     150, 166, 188, 195 *seq.*, 253
Mystic Way, 26 *seq.*, 35, 170

Neoplatonism, 54 *seq.*, 122, 134,
   139

Old Testament, 30 *seq.*
Olier, M., 205
Oratorians, 190, 195, 205
Orozco, 169
Osuna, 172
Otto, R., 32

Paracelsus, 220
Pascal, 88, 190, 206
Paul, St., 21, 29 *seq.*, 35 *seq.*, 53
   seq., 64
   his mysticism, 38
Penn, W., 223, 226
Peter Damian, St., 74
Peter of Alcantara, St., 171 *seq.*
Pier Pettignano, 93, 95, 100
Plotinus, 55, 60, 63, 222
Poiret, P., 207
Pordage, Dr., 222
Port Royal, 205
Prayer, 12, 15, 58, 82

Privity of the Passion, The, 113
Proclus, 71
Prophets, 30 *seq.*
Psalms, 30, 34 *seq.*
Purgation, 26, 41, 149, 163

Quakers, 19, 207, 219, 223 *seq.*.
   241
Quia Amore langueo, 111
Quietists, 19, 188, 191, 207 *seq.*,
   213, 223, 227

Raimondo, Fra, 155
Richard of St. Victor, 75, 80 *seq.*
Rolle, Richard, 110 *seq.*, 114 *seq.*
   Heat, sweetness and song, 117
Rowntree, W. R., 241
Ruysbroeck, 12, 51, 76, 136 *seq.*,
   148 *seq.*, 164, 204

Sadhu   Sundar   Singh,   243,
   253 *seq.*
Samuel, 30
Scale of Perfection, The, 124 *seq.*
Scheffler, J., 220
Seekers, The, 221, 223 *seq.*
Sémer, Madeleine, 242
Silesius, Angelus, 220
Simeon, Charles, 233
Slessor, Mary, 242
Soldier's Confidences with God,
   A, 240
Spiritual Marriage, 27, 184
Stäglin, Elizabeth, 145
Stephen, St., 36 *seq.*
Stuart, Mother Janet, 242
Suso, 37, 136 *seq.*, 142 *seq.*

Tauler, J., 136 *seq.*, 140 *seq.*,
   199, 220
Teresa, St., 43, 106, 164, 169,
   188, 193
   Life, 172 *seq.*
   Works, 177 *seq.*
Theologia Germanica, 139, 212

INDEX